"This book is going to be a real gem on the reading lists and bookshelves of every education and early years student, early years educator, teacher, and trainer. It is bursting at the seams with information, case studies, resources, and opportunities to reflect on current and future practice. It embodies every aspect of inclusion and discusses what this should look like in practice, and more importantly, be embedded at the core of all that we do. Stephen and Ann skilfully navigate you through each chapter, intertwining theory and examples from some of our sector's most highly regarded experts, alongside real-life case studies from Doncaster Local Authority. It is thought-provoking and challenges you to look not only at your practice, but at your thoughts, words, and beliefs and how these influence our approach to inclusion ... this will definitely be on my students' reading list and in my classrooms to support understanding of inclusion, reflection, and encourage discussion."

Helin Taylor-Greenfield, *Education and Early Years Lecturer (FE), NNEB, Pearson and LBWF Award Winner, Mental Health and Wellbeing Advocate*

"I have thoroughly enjoyed engaging with this book. Right from the start you understand the positioning of the authors and the important and powerful message they want to give. A message supported through the introduction of the Reflection Toolkit that has the child and their holistic needs at the centre. This book has so many strengths, including the style in which it is written, which makes the book accessible to a range of audiences. The use of 'voices' from practice facilitates real life examples of the Toolkit and enables the reader to reflect on how they could employ it in their work. It is empathetic, compassionate and respectful in the way it addresses issues and is particularly sensitive to the needs and feelings of parents and carers. The title on Chapter 11 about the views and aspirations of parents is spot on. How often do you ask the question 'What is your aspiration for your child?' 'How can we work together?' I valued the challenge to make us reflect on how we talk to, with and about families – their child is truly their most precious gift."

Professor Eunice Lumsden, *Head of Childhood, Youth and Families, Faculty of Health, Education and Society, University of Northampton*

T0373490

Access your Online Resources

The Inclusive Early Years Educator is accompanied by a number of printable online materials, designed to ensure this resource best supports your professional needs

Go to https://resourcecentre.routledge.com/speechmark and click on the cover of this book

Answer the question prompt using your copy of the book to gain access to the online content.

THE INCLUSIVE EARLY YEARS EDUCATOR

All young children are entitled to high-quality experiences when it comes to their education. Too often, when we meet a child who has learning differences or a disability, our instinct is to sound the alarm bells and call for additional support. *The Inclusive Early Years Educator* is a resource that encourages us to change our mindset when it comes to children with learning differences and disabilities, considering areas where our provision needs adjustment, in order to be truly inclusive.

This toolkit aims to ensure all children have the best possible chance of making progress by supporting practitioners to identify all children's strengths and to celebrate all aspects of individual children's learning. The book:

- Provides a holistic picture of a child's learning, considering an array of reflective opportunities, while always keeping the child at the centre of our thoughts.

- Includes a wealth of real-life case studies and worked examples.

- Features a diverse range of contributions from early years professionals as well as the voices of parents.

- Contains printable forms to encourage and consolidate reflections throughout the book.

- Is full of signposting and links to further resources and reading, making it an essential guide for the early years.

Some of the self-reflections will be challenging and ask us to think about aspects of our practice we may never have previously considered. With accessible guidance and strategies to advocate a change in practice based on lived experience research, *The Inclusive Early Years Educator* will enable the reader to become an ally for championing neurodiversity-affirming practice and true inclusion in early years education.

Ann Lowe is an Early Years Inclusion Officer at Doncaster Council where she provides advice, support and a range of training on inclusive practice to early years settings, schools, childminders and SENCOs. Ann has been involved in early years teaching and inclusion for 18 years in a range of roles, including a teacher of early years in schools, SENCO in school, early years advisory teacher and area SENCO.

Stephen Kilgour is a SEND advisor and spends his time providing training on various aspects of SEND and child-centred assessment. Stephen taught in schools for 15 years, including seven years as a deputy head teacher. He is also an advisor for the Foundation Stage Forum (FSF) and Tapestry.

THE INCLUSIVE EARLY YEARS EDUCATOR

A REFLECTIVE TOOLKIT

Ann Lowe

Stephen Kilgour

Routledge
Taylor & Francis Group

LONDON AND NEW YORK

Designed cover image: © Sarah Hoyle

First published 2025
by Routledge
4 Park Square, Milton Park, Abingdon, Oxon OX14 4RN

and by Routledge
605 Third Avenue, New York, NY 10158

Routledge is an imprint of the Taylor & Francis Group, an informa business

© 2025 Ann Lowe and Stephen Kilgour

The right of Ann Lowe and Stephen Kilgour to be identified as authors of this work
has been asserted in accordance with sections 77 and 78 of the Copyright, Designs
and Patents Act 1988.

All rights reserved. The purchase of this copyright material confers the right on the
purchasing institution to photocopy or download pages which bear a copyright line at
the bottom of the page. No other parts of this book may be reprinted or reproduced
or utilised in any form or by any electronic, mechanical, or other means, now known
or hereafter invented, including photocopying and recording, or in any information
storage or retrieval system, without permission in writing from the publishers.

Trademark notice: Product or corporate names may be trademarks or registered
trademarks, and are used only for identification and explanation without intent to
infringe.

British Library Cataloguing-in-Publication Data
A catalogue record for this book is available from the British Library

ISBN: 9781032529929 (hbk)
ISBN: 9781032529912 (pbk)
ISBN: 9781003409618 (ebk)

DOI: 10.4324/9781003409618

Typeset in DIN Pro
by Deanta Global Publishing Services, Chennai, India

Access the Support material: https://resourcecentre.routledge.com/speechmark

CONTENTS

PREFACE

What Does Inclusion Mean to You?

As we embarked on the project of writing this book, it was important that we took the time to reflect properly on the key word from the book's title. What does 'inclusive' mean today for our educators? What does inclusion look and feel like on a day-to-day basis in a truly outstanding setting or school? In an effort to gauge the current thoughts of those working in the sector, we posed the question on social media (X, formerly Twitter): **What Does Inclusion Mean to You?** It was great to see some of the varied and progressive responses that were offered (see Figure 0.1).

The word 'inclusion' in education has historically been linked to the way that settings or schools endeavour to cater for children with learning differences or disabilities. It felt reassuring that the responses demonstrated a widening of the scope of what high-quality inclusion actually means – particularly when we consider the complexities of the layers of disadvantage that some families might face. To embrace difference, enable belonging and provide diverse teaching strategies sounds like a great starting point for anyone considering whether they could be doing more in this area.

What does inclusion mean to you?

Making sure everyone gets what they need to thrive, grow, learn and enjoy. @KeyStageJack

Everyone feels a sense of belonging. @2202Anne

It's about belonging and your setting being 'their' space not 'your' space. @artofearlyyears

Feeling welcomed, important and respected. @gahlawatadity

A willingness to see difference positively and respond positively. @EEG_SpecialEd

Enabling children to feel like they belong. @theecleader

Providing diverse teaching strategies, creating safe spaces, & promoting collaboration among students. @EYFSBen

Inclusion is equality. @EY_KS_Anya

Being open to 'difference' - seeing it, embracing it, loving it. @EmmaLudlam2

Making our environments and practice as accessible as possible. @misssarahEYFS

#InclusiveEarlyYearsEd

FIGURE 0.1 A summary of responses from X

It is our hope that this book will provide an opportunity to widen the concept of inclusion for its readers, and we will endeavour to explore some of the key themes of inclusion that were suggested by the respondents.

Educator's View – Adity Gahlawat

Inclusion has always been a huge part of my teaching practice, more so since I started working in an international setup. I am currently working as an educator at The British School, New Delhi in India. We have around 60 different nationalities in our school, and while working and studying in such a diverse environment has various benefits and opportunities, it also is very overwhelming, especially to our learners joining the early years and primary school.

School is a space where our learners spend the majority of their day, and it is very important that they feel welcomed, respected and safe during that time.

In my class routine, I try to build mutual respect amongst all learners through various show-and-tell activities where we encourage children to bring something related to their culture or something that is very close to them, which lets them know that they are important and are being heard.

We work on individualised planning for our learners. A note is made about each child's interests and passions, and we try to source resources and toys which cater to their interests.

We also have their family photographs kept out on each child's cubbyhole, and on many occasions, I have observed children coming out of the class, looking at/hugging their pictures (especially those in Reception and Nursery, where sometimes they are not able to express that they are missing their adults at home).

Inclusion is when each child is seen and heard.

The Future of Inclusion in the Early Years

In an effort to gauge how our future early years educators felt about inclusion, we led a reflective session for the Early Years Childcare and Education (Early Years

Educator) students at Leyton Sixth Form College in London, in advance of their final two-week placement in settings. The students were given the 'Social Identity Wheel' task which was created by the University of Michigan. The activity asks participants to think about the following identities and how they impact them as individuals:

- Race
- Ethnicity
- Age
- First Language
- Sex
- Sexual Orientation
- Gender
- National Origin
- Religious or Spiritual Affiliation
- Socio-Economic Status
- Physical, Emotional, Developmental (Dis)Ability

The conversations from this diverse group of young people were refreshing and enlightening. Their ability to self-reflect with such clarity was reassuring when considering our future workforce. As a follow-up to the session, we asked the students to consider the word 'inclusion' on their final placements and to think about the positive aspects of inclusion that they see, and where settings might do better. The students spotted some familiar resources like books about different cultures and were aware that settings celebrated events such as Black History Month. Celebrations such as Eid also seemed to be embraced in the nurseries and schools they visited, with some hosting 'culture' days where parents contributed different foods for children to try. It felt from the responses that most 'inclusive practice' taking place in settings and schools was an 'add-on' rather than truly embedded practice.

The conversations exchanged with the young adults at Leyton College gave us hope that in the future the blueprint for inclusive practice might be more progressive.

Using this Toolkit

Each chapter in the book is split into three distinct parts. Stephen starts with a background section, introducing the particular focus area. Ann goes on to provide information about the way Doncaster Local Authority have implemented more progressive inclusion strategies in their early years settings and schools. Finally, workspaces are provided to help you to reflect on your own provision based on what you have read. Each form can be downloaded by following the access instructions at the front of this book so that you can use them again in the future. If you find there is not enough space on a given page, you could copy it twice or continue on the back.

What Does Inclusion Mean to You?

This could be an individual or group reflection opportunity. Use the space below to consider how you view the term 'inclusion'.

Based on these reflections, would you say that your practice is currently inclusive enough? What adjustments might be required?

Copyright material from Ann Lowe and Stephen Kilgour (2025), *The Inclusive Early Years Educator*, Routledge

ACKNOWLEDGEMENTS

We are hugely grateful to the professionals and early years educators who have inspired and contributed to this book.

Ann would like particular thanks to go to Mandy Haddock, Shelley Petta, Stephanie Douglas MBE, Anna Dougherty, Louise Hobbs, Jo Worrall, Pennie Akehurst, Ruth Churchill Dower, Laura De Cabo Seron, Brenda Cheer, Stacey Wilburn, Sarah Thurston, Alison Fleetwood, Becky Massey, Bev Downes, Leanne Webster, Sarah McMahon, Sindy Hinchliffe, Nicola Brettoner, Emma Cammack, Nicola Wosman, Tracy Outram, Lisa Hill, Sameena Choudry, Davina Sumner, Maz Cullen, Kate Ellway, Suzanne Walton, Lynne Tomlinson, Abi Kershaw, Danielle Scott and the wider Doncaster Early Years Inclusion Team.

Stephen would like to especially thank Adity Gahlawat, Jim Hoerricks PhD, Abi Miranda, Kate Moxley, Liz Pemberton, Rachna Joshi, Ben Case, Simon Wright, Kerry Murphy, Fifi Benham, Emma Pinnock, Professor Eunice Lumsden and the Education Team at Tapestry for their support and for sharing their thoughts and views.

Jules Mickleburgh has been amazingly supportive throughout the writing process, and we are both so appreciative of the time she has given to proofread the book. She has been incredibly generous with her time, as well as being a progressive ear to lend important advice.

Finally, thank you to our families who have shown encouragement and patience. Without you we wouldn't have been able to achieve this goal.

INTRODUCTION

Ann and I first started working together in 2021 following a training session that I had provided for Doncaster Local Authority. It became clear over the coming weeks and months that we had both experienced somewhat of an awakening when it came to the work we were undertaking – and also in our personal lives.

The Covid-19 pandemic had changed everything and altered the boundaries of what was considered possible. In 2019, not many people would have been able to contemplate the global shutdown that was about to occur as anything other than fantasy. On an individual level, I would have considered it unimaginable to deliver a twilight training session for 50 people in Doncaster from my spare bedroom in Newcastle. This, however, was the new reality. The way that we accessed learning had changed dramatically.

The pandemic also coincided with hugely significant global events such as the George Floyd murder, and in turn the major protests organised by the Black Lives Matter movement. Around this time, Ann and I had each started out on our anti-racism journey. We were also being exposed to a wealth of information from neurodivergent experts about the ableism that was systemic in our education system. We were inspired to explore these subjects further and consider the impact on our youngest children. It was all too apparent that over our numerous years in the education system, we hadn't spent enough time thinking about the lived experiences of those whose backgrounds were different from our own.

> **Anti-Racism** is a range of ideas and actions that aim to counter racial prejudice, systemic racism and oppression of certain racial groups.

> **Ableism** is a type of discrimination which benefits those who don't have disabilities, and therefore harms disabled people.

It would seem an appropriate time, at the beginning of this book, to lay our cards on the table, by sharing our own positionality statements. Positionality is 'the social and political context that creates your identity in terms of race, class, gender, sexuality,

DOI: 10.4324/9781003409618-1

and ability status. Positionality also describes how your identity influences, and potentially biases, your understanding of and outlook on the world' (Dictionary.com, 2018).

> **Ann***:* White, lower middle class, English speaking, cisgender female, heterosexual (married with children), university educated, able bodied, neurotypical.
> **Stephen***:* White, middle class, English speaking, cisgender male, heterosexual (married with children), university educated, able bodied, neurotypical.

This information is important to acknowledge. When we understand the influence these aspects have on our day-to-day lives, we can better understand the notion of privilege. They also help us to consider some of the significant aspects that make us who we are (there will be many additional layers). If we consider our identity in this way, it can help us to better understand the identities of the children we work with.

> **Privilege** refers to the societal advantages enjoyed by restricted groups of people – for example, male privilege, white privilege.

It is clear from our own positionality statements that we don't have the same lived experiences as many of the children we will discuss in this book. We are aware that this isn't an ideal scenario, and for this reason we will include contributions from lived experience educators or professionals throughout.

The Language We Use

Assessment of children with learning differences and disabilities can often result in a negative description of a child's development, highlighting what hasn't happened rather than focusing on the achievements a child has made. Addressing neurodivergence as a deficit rather than a strength can lead to children being viewed as incapable, which in turn can lead to lower expectations and fewer opportunities.

As a parent, reading a report about your child that only highlights the things they can't do would be soul-destroying. This is unlikely to happen for neurotypical children, so why should it be acceptable for children who have differences in the way they learn? Unfortunately, in an effort to make it clear that a child requires additional support or funding, therapists and educators will often resort to this style of writing. It is important that everyone involved in working with children understands that this approach is not fair or acceptable. If local authorities, for example, make it clear that they advocate a celebratory approach to the reporting of learning or progress, then nurseries and schools would have a better understanding of expectations.

The theory of linguistic relativity suggests that the language we use shapes the way we think and how we see the world. An example might be the fact that many people still say 'fireman' or 'policeman'. This is an example of how language can shape perception – in this instance, that the two roles mentioned are jobs for men.

In the context of education, while we continue to use language that suggests children with disabilities are problems to be fixed, we won't be able to shift to a more inclusive mindset. Terms such as 'special needs' or 'additional' needs are still widely used, but when we think more deeply about what they suggest, then it becomes obvious that they are unhelpful. A child with learning differences or a disability has the same *needs* as any other child. The need to eat, sleep, communicate, socialise and be cared for by responsive and kind adults (not an exhaustive list). It could well be construed as unfair to a child to label their needs as additional because they are neurodivergent or have a physical disability. At this time, the majority of those governing and working in education still use the term SEND (Special Educational Needs and Disability). Although the acronym isn't ideal, it is still the most recognised term when it comes to children who learn differently or have a disability. There will be instances in this book where we use 'SEND'.

Language around 'challenging behaviour' is also used commonly in education establishments and suggests that the blame is with the child. More often than not, the child is demonstrating a level of distress or unhappiness. As educators, we need to be considerate of how our environment and provision contributes to a child's ability to regulate their emotions. There has been a marked uptake in the use of terms like 'self-regulation' and, just as importantly, 'co-regulation' across the early years sector over recent years; with appropriate understanding, this must be viewed as progression, particularly if it means a move away from behaviour sanctions and shaming practices of children who are under 5 years old.

Self-regulation refers to our ability to manage our responses and reactions to feelings and things that may be happening to us.

Co-regulation refers to the way parents or key people in a child's life support them to self-regulate. This may be through calming words or actions and generally being 'present' in the moment of stress. This co-regulation helps a child become more adept at their own self-regulation skills over time.

Throughout this book, we attempt to use language that we deem to be progressive, avoiding where possible the terms 'special needs' or 'additional needs'. We have no doubt that over time the themes and language in this book may well become outdated. However, we will both endeavour to continue to consider the preferences of individuals as well as the wider neurodivergent/disabled communities as we navigate our own learning journeys.

The Reflection Toolkit

As we learned more about ableism from the neurodivergent professionals we were lucky enough to meet or engage with, we became increasingly aware that as an education sector, when we encounter children who are different, we have historically

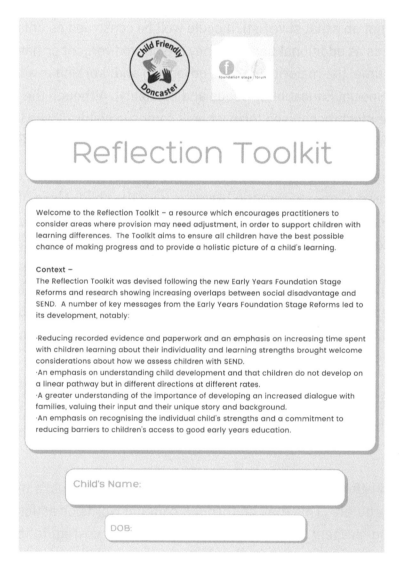

FIGURE 0.2 The front cover of the Reflection Toolkit

attempted to 'fix' them so they can appear to be more 'normal'. Emily Lees is an Autistic Speech and Language Therapist and she gives the following example: 'An Autistic child who needs ear defenders due to their hypersensitivity to noise is told to wear them less so that they can 'get used to' the noise.' (Lees, 2022, p.4). Another scenario might be that an Autistic child has been given a target to increase the amount of eye contact they make while they communicate. In both of these examples, the school/setting/authority is valuing 'normality' over suffering. It is society's responsibility to adjust and accept differences, and we should be championing this notion in the early years.

After many discussions, we came up with a concept for a new type of assessment tool for early years settings and schools in Doncaster that would support their work with children who had learning differences or disabilities. The key aim of the Reflection Toolkit was for settings and schools to consider a child holistically and then adjust their provision, rather than trying to mould the child into something they were not.

The intention was that when a nursery or school met a child with learning differences or a disability for the first time, rather than the first port of call being a request for support, instead they would take a step back and consider what adjustments were possible to improve access. When we meet any child for the first time, we need to devote the majority of our energy to learning as much as we can about them. This ensures that we can plan around their interests and avoid situations and activities that make them feel anxious or unhappy. Ultimately, a happy and engaged child is going to make progress.

The Reflection Toolkit is made up of the following sections:

- Basic Needs
- Wellbeing and Involvement Guidance
- Inclusive Practice
- Characteristics of Effective Teaching and Learning
- Communication
- Schematic Play
- Executive Function
- Sensory Reflection
- Child's Voice
- Parent's Views and Aspirations
- Holistic Reflection Overview

- Goals
- Progress Towards Outcomes
- Actions

We envisaged that upon meeting a child who required additional support, a nursery or school would use the Reflection Toolkit for a 'baseline' period of approximately six weeks, during which time they would seek to find out as much as possible about the child in question.

The actual resource can be printed or completed as an editable PDF (freely available to download by scanning Figure 0.3).

An educator can make regular notes in the document over the agreed timeframe. Once the various sections have been completed, there is an opportunity to set key goals that would significantly benefit the child – this may be to use an alternative communication system, or to gain the confidence to explore the learning environment independently. Regardless of the goals, it is important that the child's family's views and opinions are valued throughout and that concerted efforts are made to establish high-quality relationships with the central people in the child's life.

It is no coincidence that the sections of the toolkit match up neatly with the chapter list for this book. We were approached by the publisher to create a more expansive 'workbook' that provided the opportunity to delve much more deeply into the subject areas, while providing even more opportunity for reflection. We are thrilled to have this opportunity, and hope that as a sector we can become as genuinely inclusive as possible and set the standard for other stages to follow. Each chapter in *The Inclusive Early Years Educator* contains a case study of a setting or school in Doncaster that has implemented changes based on their own use of the Reflection Toolkit.

FIGURE 0.3 A QR code to download the Reflection Toolkit

References

Dictionary.com (2018) 'Positionality'. Dictionary.com. www.dictionary.com/e/gender-sexuality/positionality

Lees, E. (2022) 'A Beginner's Guide to Ableism'. Tapestry. https://tapestry.info/a-beginners-guide-to-ableism.html

Chapter 1

ESTABLISHING A CHILD-CENTRED APPROACH TO REQUESTS FOR SUPPORT AND FUNDING

Reforms to the Early Years Foundation Stage (EYFS) in England came into effect in September 2021. They followed a year in which more than 3,000 schools took part in a pilot where they were 'Early Adopters'.

The changes to the EYFS statutory framework were made to:

- improve outcomes at age 5, particularly in early language and literacy
- reduce workload such as unnecessary paperwork, so you can spend more time with the children in your care.

One aspect of reducing workload links to a practice which became commonplace across the sector. The 2012 version of Development Matters had, in many cases, become a bank of statements that educators were marking off and evidencing in order to accurately place a child in one of six age bands (even though the guidance stated clearly on almost every page that it was not to be used as a checklist). The proliferation of online learning journals in the years that followed enabled educators to neatly gather huge quantities of photos and videos for each child in their setting and use these to help them come to a conclusion about the progress a child had made. There were, of course, numerous benefits brought by this new technology, perhaps the most important being the ability to easily share moments of learning between home and nursery/school and vice versa.

Considering the numbers of children each adult is responsible for in a group, it soon becomes apparent how these assessment and tracking practices can easily spiral out of control, creating an unmanageable workload, particularly when added to the

DOI: 10.4324/9781003409618-2

range of other responsibilities that are part of any educator's role. Although the response to the reforms in the EYFS haven't been overwhelmingly positive, the notion of eliminating excessive assessment processes seems to have been well received in the main.

Why Was it Happening?

Although evidencing each statement from Development Matters was time-consuming for practitioners, many were disappointed that these systems were changing. The child development information contained within the document had for the best part of ten years been a valuable asset for many of the EY workforce, but had in reality become a crutch for many of those working in the sector, particularly those who had qualified during that time. In the past, the National Nursery Examination Board qualification meant that the level of child development input for prospective educators was vast, with varied and numerous placement opportunities. This led to nursery nurses who had a deep understanding of typical milestones in a child's formative years. As qualification requirements changed and the content of courses adjusted, child development documents like Development Matters became go-to resources for inexperienced staff. One of the key suggestions during the EYFS reforms was that those working in the EYFS needed enhanced access to high-quality continuing professional development (CPD): 'Providers must support staff to undertake appropriate training and professional development opportunities to ensure they offer quality learning and development experiences for children that continually improves' (DfE, 2023). This was in part to enable a departure from such a reliance on child development documentation, and a shift towards professional judgement.

The gathering of information linked to statements from Development Matters was also invariably a means for leaders/managers to demonstrate the extent of progress that the children had made over the time they had been attending a given setting or school. The spectre of a visit from an inspection body such as Ofsted was generally the driving force for such practice. Requesting and producing data of this type is somewhat understandable. It can be presented in a clear and concise manner while being easy to understand and quick to absorb. For those who need to make judgements on quality, having something quantifiable can be particularly helpful. It might be that the governing board of an education establishment wants a snapshot of how 'well' the nursery or school is doing, and doesn't have time for long paragraphs of descriptive language.

What Is Wrong with Producing Data?

The purpose of data production is generally to 'show' how well our children are progressing. If we can mark off the majority of statements within a given curriculum area and age band, then we can confidently say that they are 'secure' in that area. If we have this information to hand at various points throughout the year (data drops, anyone?!), then we can 'track' a child's progress over time. Even better, we can then make judgements about cohorts of children by comparing their progress and producing more data that details the percentage of children who are seemingly making good progress. This all sounds ideal, until we consider the negative impacts.

When our assessment systems are driven by the need for copious amounts of evidence of a child's learning, linked to a lengthy list of statements, then it would be impossible for this not to impact our day-to-day practice when working with children. Under the previous assessment systems, it was common for an educator to have a target of observations/assessments that they needed to hit each week. Considering that the heart of our provision in the EYFS should be child-led learning and choice making, the potential for contradiction is fairly clear. If I know, for instance, that on a given day I need to get a photo or video of a particular child writing letters from his or her name, the chances are that the circumstances that will lead to the recording will be disingenuous. They are also unlikely to have involved a child making choices about their learning in that particular moment. Perhaps the most powerful consideration in these circumstances is 'Could anything more purposeful and engaging have been happening instead?' If the adult in question could have been freed up at that moment to observe and connect with children rather than hiding behind a tablet, how much more learning may have occurred?

At a leadership or management level, the amount of time spent processing the information to create the data can also be huge. If this time could be reinvested in focusing on adapting provision in response to the unique group of children in their care, then surely quality will be significantly enhanced. After all, if provision is outstanding, then progress should be the same. Provided we are continually reflecting and adjusting our provision based on our observations (both informal and formal), the majority of our children should continue to make very good progress.

What Might Alternatives Look Like?

If we are to abandon data-centric approaches, then we must have solid systems in place to ensure our assessment is robust and, most importantly, identifies the children in the group who may need extra support. Without standardised criteria based on a child development document, in the first instance we need to ensure that our staff teams have appropriate input to provide them with the confidence to make judgements about children's learning. That is not to say that reference materials aren't useful, but we should be moving away from a place where one assessment resource is our be-all and end-all. Realistically, focusing on the way in which the children are or are not engaging within the classroom environment can often be the biggest indicator of learning.

Once there is satisfaction that educators within a setting or school are using their observations and interactions to accurately make judgements about children's learning (this should ideally be a collaborative process), then we need to have processes that help us to more specifically monitor those children who are not accessing the provision in the way that we would hope. Informal discussions about progress should be taking place among team members on a daily basis, but there should also be more formal arrangements to make sure that no children are slipping through the net. These might look like the following:

- A six-weekly progress meeting to discuss children who are not thriving in the environment, preferably broken down into the various curriculum areas.
- At a leadership level, an awareness of actions/next steps following these meetings is essential.
- If it has been identified that a child is not accessing our provision as we would hope, and therefore not making the progress we would expect, then there must be a 'So what are we going to do about it?' reflection.

If a leadership team or a board of governors is intent on analysing quantifiable figures, then the number of 'concerns' we have around our children's access to their environment could easily be monitored. The hope would obviously be that this number would come down over time, demonstrating the impact of the adjustments that have been made.

SEND Assessment

Assessment of children with learning differences and disabilities has been a substantial topic of conversation in the aftermath of the reforms. As welcome as a shift away from an evidence-heavy workload is, there has been much confusion as to how childminders, nurseries and schools are now expected to categorise quite how significant a child's support needs are.

Unfortunately, this has created a scenario whereby, in many areas of the country, the expectation is that we should still be using the previous assessment approach for children who need extra support. In this way, local authorities can allocate funding based on the age bands from the previous incarnation of Development Matters (or a comparative checklist-style document). Although understandable in terms of straightforward evidence-based decision making, the idea that these children are not entitled to child-centred assessment like their peers seems grossly unfair. The quality of input that this group will receive will be negatively impacted by a need to document each and every developmental milestone that they encounter. This obviously throws up the same concerns regarding workload and purposeful use of time that have already been mentioned. Added to this, the fact that the vast majority of developmental reference materials are based upon typical developmental pathways means that, in many circumstances, the milestones or 'targets' that these children are working towards may not be appropriate at all. There need to be more progressive systems in place to ensure that children's day-to-day learning is not negatively impacted by the requirements of people or panels who make these very important decisions about levels of support or funding.

There is a wealth of assessment tools available to educators, and new resources are being created all the time – often by people who are hoping for a way to easily categorise the level of support a child will need. The challenge with adopting any new assessment tool is to ensure we use them in a way that centres the child. The same assessment tool can be used well by one educator but inappropriately by another. In my opinion, if you are using any assessment tool with the sole aim of creating data to satisfy someone else's requirements, then it is very unlikely to be a child-centred approach.

Cherry Garden School created a free assessment framework based on six main Branch Maps. These one-page documents can be printed and used to enable discussions in settings and schools about children's learning and appropriate next steps. The intention is that they are used flexibly to monitor development, with no expectation that any two children will progress in the same way.

The Branch Maps can be downloaded by scanning Figure 1.1.

FIGURE 1.1 A QR code to download the Cherry Garden Branch Maps

Developing a Reflective Approach to Assessment in Doncaster

Every child can make progress with the right support.

(DfE, Development Matters, 2023, p.5)

The Pen Green document 'A Celebratory Approach to Working with Children with SEND', published in September 2021, provided an opportunity to review our thinking and approach in Doncaster. We were on a profound journey to learn more about neurodiversity and made a commitment to developing a neurodiversity-affirming approach to all aspects of our early years work.

We began to develop the Reflection Toolkit in the months prior to the EYFS reforms, and the emphasis of the toolkit embraced the notion that the unique profile of all children should be recognised as strengths to be supported and built on. The toolkit considered a range of areas and advocated that actions and adjustments to provision for a child should be based on in-depth knowledge and understanding of an individual child's abilities, rejecting the concept that all children should be assessed against typical developmental milestones.

My Doncaster colleagues embraced this approach. They felt, as I did, that using assessment tools based on typical development for neurodivergent children had been inappropriate for some time and that using this approach was out of date and disheartening for themselves and parents. With this in mind, colleagues were keen to reform the way we used assessment. The aforementioned Pen Green document reinforced what we had already imagined: that assessment for neurodivergent children should have the flexibility to move in a very different direction. Consideration of assessment tools then evolved into conversations about the request process for additional early years funding. In Doncaster, we began to, and are continuing to, develop our principles and practice to advocate a neurodiversity-affirming approach to the requesting and allocation of funding.

Promoting Child-Centred Approaches to Funding

The key strand we were keen to embed throughout the request process was that funding should be used and requested to advocate and deliver a child-centred approach. Requests for funding or Early Years Inclusion Team support have traditionally outlined the learning 'difficulties' a child presents with and how they are unable to access aspects of the setting's routine or provision due to these 'difficulties'. This centres the support on aspects of conformity or strategies to 'help' the child present as neurotypical. Funding was often being used to help the child to access routines that may be assumed to be beneficial for typically developing children and the adults managing the child in the setting, but not necessarily meaningful to the individual child. A shift in thinking was required to focus on the strengths of the child and what would enable them to make steps of progress in the most appropriate individual direction.

A shift of this type was initially difficult and challenging to implement, particularly when quality early years provision has been based purely on neurotypical learning styles for so long. When we ask the question 'Is this conformity-centred or child-centred?' I often see practitioners experiencing 'lightbulb' moments. Moving the ownership of the 'difficulties' away from the child and focusing on the provision is a game changer. A recent meeting with a setting highlighted the challenges and benefits in moving to this approach.

I was involved in supporting the school in question which was struggling to meet the needs of a child they had identified with SEND. The child was currently receiving some additional Early Intervention Allowance and attended 15 hours. The teachers were reaching their limit in trying to support the child to access the provision. Conversations included comments such as 'They can't access the provision without 1:1 support – they tip out boxes without using provision purposely' and 'The funding we get isn't enough, we need 1:1 all the time'. It was becoming increasingly evident from our discussions that funding was being used to try to teach the child to be more neurotypical, not develop their own individual strengths and learning outcomes. This was putting increasing pressures on the educators and the child. As I began to discuss the child's outcomes with the team, we reflected on:

- Does the outcome advocate a child-centred approach?
- Is funding being used to move the child on to the next steps in their individual learning journey?
- Are we approaching the outcomes with neurodivergent considerations, or are we using the funding to affirm neurodiversity?
- Does the outcome centre on the provision available in the setting and how a child can fit into this, rather than considering how the funding can support a child to develop on their own journey?
- Is a child's individual neurodivergent learning profile considered?
- Are we attempting to make a child appear more neurotypical?

The lightbulb moment came when the practitioner described the levels of engagement of the child when accessing the carpet time routine, which was where the additional funding support was currently being focused. It emerged that the child was particularly passive during these experiences or showing levels of distress. We then discussed what we had observed and noticed about the child's interests, and how the additional funding/enhanced ratios and outcomes could be planned to develop moments of shared communication and joy in areas of provision where the child showed heightened levels of engagement. Using the funding in a child-centred manner could pave the way for increased progress and increased levels of engagement – an outcome they were all much happier with.

> One of the roles of education is to awaken and develop these powers of creativity. Instead, what we have is a culture of standardisation.
>
> (Sir Ken Robinson, May 2013)

Reflecting on Documentation

Passionate and committed to child-centred approaches to funding, Mandy Haddock (Early Years Inclusion Officer Lead for SEND and Early Inclusion Allowance Funding) reviewed documentation to remove the expectation for settings to provide assessment information related to typical ages and stages. Previous to the reforms, age bands related to development matters were required as part of the request process. Assessment information in relation to individual outcomes is now encouraged, affirming a child-centred approach.

Mandy also developed the request documentation to include an 'All About Me' sheet which gives information about the child's strengths and interests in an effort to make the process more individualised. This sheet aligns with the aspects of the Reflection Toolkit focusing on the strengths of the individual child. As part of the request for additional funding, providers were also asked to describe when the child was most engaged and involved in learning using aspects such as scales of involvement and placing emphasis on the importance of the characteristics of effective learning.

Reforming the documentation to advocate a child-centred approach then began to open conversations with partner services such as the Educational Psychology Service and Health partners as this was a different way of assessing children and recognising the support they needed.

Transition documentation, which previously focused on levels of attainment, was also carefully considered and reviewed. A focus was placed on the individual interests and strengths of the child. Sections such as 'What's great about me?' provided a framework for the document to celebrate all aspects of the child as opposed to concerns and difficulties.

The Integrated Progress Check also had an overhaul. My colleague Shelley Petta, Early Years Inclusion Officer and Assessment Lead, worked closely with health colleagues to develop a new two-year progress check to identify children's strengths and highlight where there were concerns about a child's *progress*, rather than about their *attainment*. Shifting to this model served as a reflective moment for the setting and a consideration of what they were providing for the child, not how the child presented in relation to typically developing children.

Shelley describes the process of how the Integrated Progress Check evolved, working in partnership with health colleagues:

Developing a celebratory approach to assessment prompted a review of the Integrated Progress Check. The document was changed to include photographs and video clips from parents representing an increasingly holistic picture of the child. These changes gave Doncaster providers the opportunity to engage parents despite the barriers that may be faced, providing an all-round more authentic and therefore valid understanding of the child's strengths and areas where, as a team, the setting, health and parents could support the child in areas for development.

The key to reviewing and developing the Integrated Progress Check was ensuring that it was celebratory. Had the child made progress since being in setting? Did the strategies put in place by the setting to support the child work? If not, what did the parents/setting need to do differently to build in success?

The celebratory document was designed to enable honest and open conversations from a strengths-based standpoint. Difficult conversations can be held when a parent feels that their child has been truly 'seen'.

Shelley Petta (Early Years Inclusion Officer,
Lead for Integrated Progress Check)

We hoped to weave the unique qualities of every child through each stage of documentation used by early years providers.

Reflecting on Language Used to Describe Support

In Doncaster's Early Years Inclusion Team and when working with providers, we have tried hard to drop the term 'one-to-one' (1:1). I hold my hand up: I myself have used the term in the past to demonstrate the significance of a child's needs until I learned more and reflected upon my own practice.

The term is questionable and in need of review, particularly when considering neurodiversity-affirming practice. It needs further investigation when used. Are we suggesting a child is unable to function without an adult to support or that an adult is needed to ensure a child is developing in a neurotypical way? Is an adult supporting a child to conform to existing routines devised for neurotypical children? When delving further into this topic with educators, they often describe aspects of typical development which they are struggling to engage a neurodivergent child in (e.g. group time and phonics). The key is to use a child-centred approach when considering support needed.

Mandy Haddock (Early Years Inclusion Officer, Lead for SEND) keenly reframes this language, when used, and reminds educators that funding is for enhancing ratios to enable support and independence.

It's important to consider:

- Does the child benefit from 1:1 support all the time?
- How does this support children in developing their independence and self-advocacy?
- Do we think of needing 1:1 support for children in order for them to better present as neurotypical?
- Is a request for 1:1 based on a child needing support to fit into the setting or for the setting to foster a sense of belonging for the child?

In moving away from this term and practice, we need to gain a deeper understanding of the importance of honouring the differences of neurodivergent children and how to plan provision that promotes independence and values a child's unique learning profile.

Traditional requests for support and funding describe a child with a predominantly deficit narrative and spell out what support the child needs to access routines and provision which is set up for the neuro-majority, essentially reinforcing the notion that a child needs 1:1 support to teach them to appear more neurotypical.

An essential starting point to begin provision mapping is developing our knowledge about the child's strengths, interests and learning profile. This is where the Reflection Toolkit is a useful tool, supporting the mapping of provision so that it is tailored around developing the child's strengths and authentic play.

Initially, it is important to consider when a child shows strength in their independent skills. This would usually be when a child shows high levels of involvement, wellbeing and self-regulation. At these times during the day, the child will increase their self-directed learning, potentially needing less or no 1:1 adult support during these parts of the session. An example of this from a school visit can be seen below.

Seth is a 3-year-old boy accessing nursery for 15 hours a week. Seth shows high levels of wellbeing in the outdoor area. Seth is particularly interested in running and loves outdoor construction materials, especially tyres and boxes. Seth will often position himself with the tyres or within crates or boxes and enjoys climbing in and out of them. Seth is also interested in the outdoor water area and particularly enjoys jumping in puddles, using the water butt to fill up containers and using the hosepipe.

The educators had identified that another seven children show particular interest in the outdoor water area. The team set about planning a timetable based upon increased access to the outdoor water area with two adults working with a group of children – a mixture of neurotypical and neurodivergent individuals. The plan involved the scaffolding of the group's individual targets in mathematics, communication and literacy in the water area outside. In-depth knowledge of the children was used to support interactions, and intended learning experiences could move in different directions for each individual child.

This way of planning provision advocates learning that can move in any direction, embracing engagement and giving value to all types of play. There is no capping of learning, only a range of possibilities that can be supported through the environment, resources provided and the connections between child and child or child and adult. Fostering a sense of belonging for neurodivergent children is essential to developing a culture of child-centred provision. The expectation that if children learn differently, then they need additional adult support to access education is an accepted one, not only within schools and settings but in the wider communities we serve. We may hear educators or parents commenting on neurodivergent children with statements such as 'they need someone with them'.

The question is how do we demonstrate what education looks like for *all* children, not just what education looks like for neurotypical children? Only by increasing awareness and understanding of neurodiversity do we begin to make a move away from ableism and the idea that children with SEND are a problem to be fixed. This requires everyone in a setting and school to embrace *difference* not difficulty, *strengths* not deficits, and to become confident in challenging discriminatory, ableist practice.

In Doncaster, we are beginning to develop an understanding of difference not being a deficit through conversations with Portage families, family hubs and the many educators we work with every day. A good starting point for these conversations is to use texts and books with children which describe disability positively or embrace neurodivergence as a strength. Texts such as *Loud!*, *Talking Is Not My Thing* and *Me and My Sister* by author Rose Robbins have proven useful access points for positive discussions about disability and neurodiversity. They can add to the sense of belonging for children – they can identify: 'That character is like me!' – and difference should be celebrated.

Reflecting on How Funding Can Be Used

It's no secret that SEND support for children in the UK is grossly underfunded. Settings and schools are understandably frustrated at the lack of financial support for inclusion. In a cost-of-living crisis, the new childcare funding entitlement from April 2024 and with increased referrals for SEND support, huge investment is needed in this area. Reconsidering and reframing language around the need for 1-1 support for a child does not result in needing less funding. Enhancing provision still requires increased adults and planned support. We are where we are, as the saying goes, so how do we balance the books with very little financial support?

Some possible starting points:

- How much funding do I actually have?
- Explore all possible amounts: Nursery Education Funding allocated for each individual child, Pupil Premium funding if entitled, Disability Access Funding if entitled and any additional Inclusion funding allocated to the individual child.
- What are the child's personalised learning outcomes and how will I deploy adults to meet these?

- Based upon what money I have, what can I afford in terms of adults and support?
- What experiences and provision do I need to provide for the individual child? Are there any other children's learning outcomes that can be fostered using similar experiences?
- What do my existing routines look like and how can these be adapted?
- How do I develop a routine to ensure the child has increased access to experiences where they show increasing independence?
- How do we develop a community of support and flexibility through supporting the learning of groups of children, including the individual child?

Reflecting on Strengths-Based Language and Funding Requests

Traditionally, requests for funding have asked for detailed descriptions of the problems, difficulties and delays children have with their learning and development. I have spent many, many hours over my career filling in paperwork detailing all the things a child can't do, to create a stark picture that will hopefully result in SEND panel members recognising how 'challenging' the child is so that they can throw a significant sum of money at the 'problem'.

In the Doncaster Early Years Inclusion Team, we started to dismantle this approach, working to flip the narrative by providing descriptions of children's strengths and unique character rather than describing problems. This has come with its challenges, as the internalised ableism of the system has been entrenched in this practice for so long. It is enlightening to request support using non-deficit language, but it also takes a lot of practice. I find that we can revert so quickly to our old ways of describing weaknesses and problems as we believe the panel won't necessarily give us the support we need unless we describe the child in a negative way. I remember distinctly my colleague Mandy Haddock (Early Years Inclusion Officer, Lead for SEND) excitedly sharing with me that she had written a request for an Education Health and Care plan using strengths-based language, a significant shift in promoting a neurodiversity-affirming language in our procedures and an exhilarating moment for Mandy. We discussed the differences in writing in this way and were agreed in our commitment to promoting it.

I used the following example as part of a training session in promoting strengths-based language at the beginning of the autumn term in 2021. In all honesty, it took twice as long for me to write the strengths-based description as the deficit version. I recognised that this is because I, like so many of us, am all too well practised in describing 'difficulties'.

Reflecting on Deficit Descriptions

- Sam is 4 years old. Sam becomes distressed in noisy environments and will become upset without his ear defenders.
- Sam is non-verbal and will become upset during transitions due to his difficulties in understanding – for example, coming inside from outside. This often results in him throwing himself to the floor or screaming.
- Sam has sensory difficulties and will immerse himself in water and often try to drink water from the water tray or the hosepipe outside.
- Sam has no awareness of danger and will climb on objects and jump off from unsafe heights.
- Sam is fixated on songs on his tablet and becomes upset if an adult puts on a different programme.
- Sam has repetitive play and will move a car up and down in the same directions.
- Sam finds it difficult to access activities and needs objects of reference to help him to understand where to play and what to do.

Promoting Strengths-Based Descriptions

- Sam is 4 years old. Sam enjoys quiet spaces, particularly outside where he enjoys running, jumping, water play, exploring wind/nature and vehicle play. Sam shows he is excited by outdoor activities such as exploring the water and feeling the wind by jumping up and down, moving his hands and arms in a rapid motion and making high-pitched sounds and babbling.
- Sam shows an interest in small world play and enjoys moving cars up and down tracks. Sam makes choices by pointing or gesturing towards objects he is presented with. Sam shows an interest in electronic resources such as tablets and phones and can access his favourite songs by choosing the correct icon on the tablet.
- Sam benefits from being shown objects to help him understand transitions – for example, being shown a plate to come inside and access his snack.
- Sam benefits from wearing his ear defenders in noisy environments.

The example had almost everyone in the room nodding their heads, questioning their practice and reflecting on why our systems had been so negative and detrimental to children with SEND in the past. Practitioners from across Doncaster agreed it was high time we started to talk about neurodivergent children positively and embrace difference. For a moment, it felt as though we were trailblazers, ready to change ableist practice.

There was, of course, a range of challenges from delegates – reflections such as 'It's a nice idea, but how will we ever get the money we need if we describe children in this way?' and 'It's difficult to recognise the child has a problem if you don't describe it.' All important points to reflect on. In a cost-of-living and recruitment crisis, cash-strapped settings and schools are already struggling to be financially sustainable. The anxiety of not being allocated funding by changing the approach was understandable a concern. Listening and understanding to these pressures is vital if we are to collectively make the shift. In Doncaster, we are still on that journey of bringing about change and understanding.

A summary of Doncaster's child-centred support and funding request processes can be found in Figure 1.2.

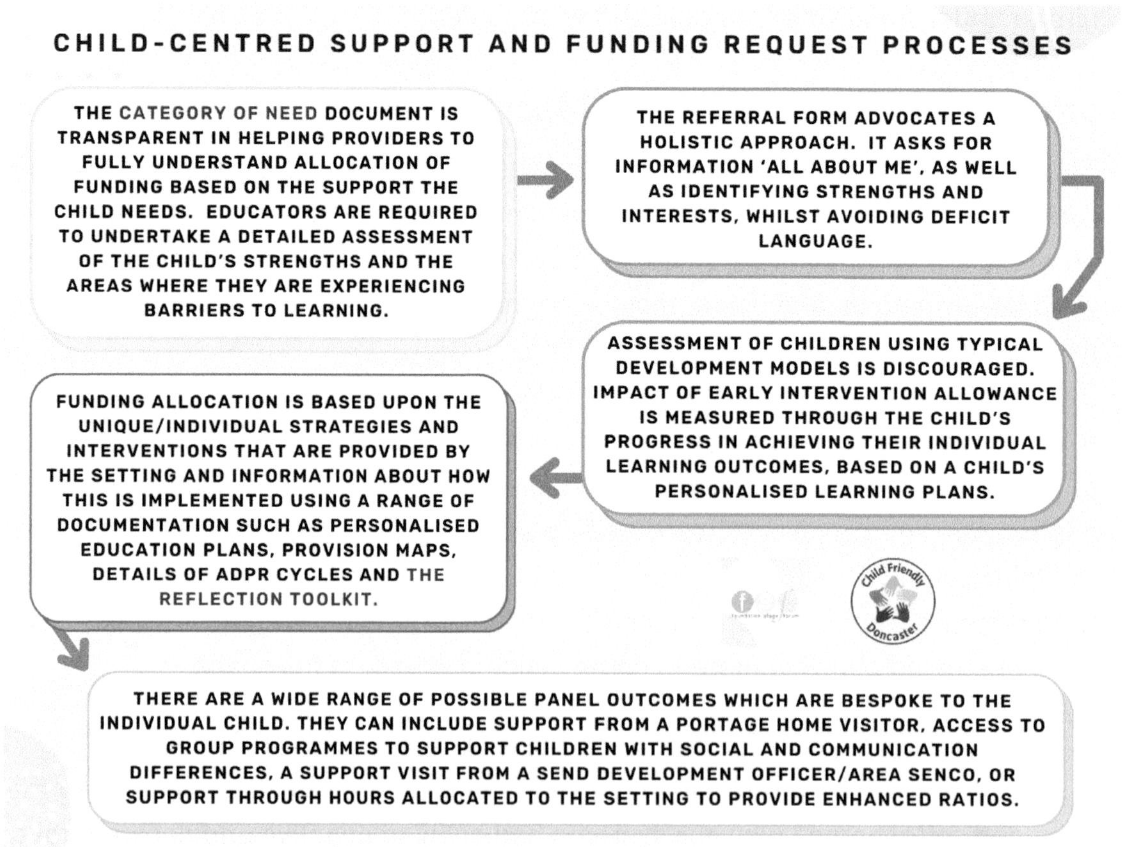

CHILD-CENTRED SUPPORT AND FUNDING REQUEST PROCESSES

THE CATEGORY OF NEED DOCUMENT IS TRANSPARENT IN HELPING PROVIDERS TO FULLY UNDERSTAND ALLOCATION OF FUNDING BASED ON THE SUPPORT THE CHILD NEEDS. EDUCATORS ARE REQUIRED TO UNDERTAKE A DETAILED ASSESSMENT OF THE CHILD'S STRENGTHS AND THE AREAS WHERE THEY ARE EXPERIENCING BARRIERS TO LEARNING.

THE REFERRAL FORM ADVOCATES A HOLISTIC APPROACH. IT ASKS FOR INFORMATION 'ALL ABOUT ME', AS WELL AS IDENTIFYING STRENGTHS AND INTERESTS, WHILST AVOIDING DEFICIT LANGUAGE.

ASSESSMENT OF CHILDREN USING TYPICAL DEVELOPMENT MODELS IS DISCOURAGED. IMPACT OF EARLY INTERVENTION ALLOWANCE IS MEASURED THROUGH THE CHILD'S PROGRESS IN ACHIEVING THEIR INDIVIDUAL LEARNING OUTCOMES, BASED ON A CHILD'S PERSONALISED LEARNING PLANS.

FUNDING ALLOCATION IS BASED UPON THE UNIQUE/INDIVIDUAL STRATEGIES AND INTERVENTIONS THAT ARE PROVIDED BY THE SETTING AND INFORMATION ABOUT HOW THIS IS IMPLEMENTED USING A RANGE OF DOCUMENTATION SUCH AS PERSONALISED EDUCATION PLANS, PROVISION MAPS, DETAILS OF ADPR CYCLES AND THE REFLECTION TOOLKIT.

THERE ARE A WIDE RANGE OF POSSIBLE PANEL OUTCOMES WHICH ARE BESPOKE TO THE INDIVIDUAL CHILD. THEY CAN INCLUDE SUPPORT FROM A PORTAGE HOME VISITOR, ACCESS TO GROUP PROGRAMMES TO SUPPORT CHILDREN WITH SOCIAL AND COMMUNICATION DIFFERENCES, A SUPPORT VISIT FROM A SEND DEVELOPMENT OFFICER/AREA SENCO, OR SUPPORT THROUGH HOURS ALLOCATED TO THE SETTING TO PROVIDE ENHANCED RATIOS.

FIGURE 1.2 A summary of Doncaster's child-centred support and funding request processes

Thought Provocations

- Why do you assess in the way that you do?
- Is your assessment taking place to enhance outcomes for children, or to provide information to someone who is interested?
- If you are unhappy about assessment demands that are being made of you, have you voiced concerns?

References

Department for Education (2023) Development Matters. https://assets.publishing.service.gov.uk/government/uploads/system/uploads/attachment_data/file/1180056/DfE_Development_Matters_Report_Sep2023.pdf

Department for Education (2023) Early years foundation stage (EYFS) Statutory framework. www.gov.uk/government/publications/early-years-foundation-stage-framework--2

Pen Green Centre (2021) A Celebratory Approach to Working with Children with SEND. www.pengreen.org/a-celebratory-approach-to-working-with-children-with-send

Robinson, K. (2013) How to escape education's death valley. TED. www.youtube.com/watch?v=wX78iKhInsc

Chapter 2

BASIC NEEDS

Developing a Reflective Approach to Basic Needs in Doncaster

As an educator, it can be helpful in many scenarios to consider yourself in a situation a child is facing, in an effort to better understand why they might be presenting or responding in a certain way. This can be a relatively straightforward exercise when it comes to the basic physiological needs that we all share. Let's think about how changes in these basic needs might make us feel.

- **Food.** How does a lack of food affect our day-to-day emotions? If we have missed a meal, does it impact our ability to focus and concentrate? Or are you the type of person who can become 'hangry' (feeling angry because of hunger)? Maybe we have eaten too much or the wrong type of food, which leaves us feeling sluggish and sleepy. As we grow and mature, we generally understand that having healthy eating routines can positively impact our ability to perform well in our work and play.
- **Drink.** Similarly to a lack of food, a lack of fluids can negatively affect our ability to function effectively. Most of us have been in situations where dehydration has led us to be desperate for a cold drink. Whether it is after exercise or due to hot weather, when we feel thirsty, it can become hard to think about anything else. Once the dehydration increases, we can feel weak or faint and experience side effects such as headaches – all messages from our body that we need a drink!
- **Clothing.** Living in the UK, it is commonplace to misjudge the weather. The middle of summer is no guarantee that a jumper won't be required, and an unusually mild day in the winter can leave us feeling that we've worn far too much. To be in a situation where we feel too cold or too hot can leave us feeling distracted. Our ability to focus on tasks at hand can be significantly impaired by our body's responses to such experiences.
- **Sleep.** Any new parent will tell you that one of the most challenging aspects of life with a baby is a lack of sleep. Attempting to function at work, for example, after a very broken night can be extremely difficult, especially when you are fully aware

DOI: 10.4324/9781003409618-3

that the following night is likely to bring similar challenges. Other scenarios that many will have experienced – such as jet lag or going into work after a late night – can lead to difficulties carrying out the most simple of tasks.

The ability to communicate and address basic physiological needs is hugely important. As adults, we can usually ensure that we don't regularly suffer negative consequences due to these requirements. That is not to say that at different stages of our lives we will not encounter consistent challenges linked to any one of them. Life events such as a significant illness might be the cause, but unfortunately low pay or poor working conditions can also create scenarios where educators are forced to think about these needs more than they would like. As much as the main focus of this workbook is on the needs of the children in our care, we are keen for practitioner wellbeing to also be at the forefront of reflective practice. It isn't necessarily easy, but to communicate challenges linked to these areas to an understanding friend or colleague can be helpful in seeking appropriate support.

Maslow's Hierarchy of Needs

If you have come across Abraham Maslow's work, the notion of basic physiological needs is likely to sound familiar. In 1943, the American psychologist wrote the paper 'A Theory of Human Motivation'. Maslow proposed that there was a 'Hierarchy of Needs', which is often displayed as a pyramid. At the base of the pyramid are the most fundamental physiological needs; once these are met, the safety needs take precedence, and so on.

Maslow described the sections of the hierarchy as follows:

The 'physiological' needs. The needs that are usually taken as the starting point for motivation theory are the so-called physiological drives …
    The safety needs. If the physiological needs are relatively well gratified, there then emerges a new set of needs, which we may categorize roughly as the safety needs …
    The love needs. If both the physiological and the safety needs are fairly well gratified, then there will emerge the love and affection and belongingness needs …
    The esteem needs. All people in our society … have a need or desire for a stable, firmly based, (usually) high evaluation of themselves, for self-respect, or self-esteem, and for the esteem of others …
    The need for self-actualization. Even if all these needs are satisfied, we may still often (if not always) expect that a new discontent and restlessness will soon develop, unless the individual is doing what he is fitted for. A musician must make

music, an artist must paint, a poet must write, if he is to be ultimately happy. What a man *can* be, he *must* be. This need we may call self-actualization.

(Maslow, 1943)

The ideas contained within Maslow's work are still considered by many to be relevant and valuable, but there are professionals who feel that the model is problematic. In his book *Social: Why Our Brains Are Wired to Connect*, Matthew Lieberman (2015) explains that the latest science actually suggests that our social bonds are the most crucial need we have. He gives the example of a baby who is completely dependent on others, with no means to find food or shelter for survival. As early years educators, we are acutely aware not only of the need to care for our youngest children by providing for their basic physiological needs, but also the vital requirement to support their social and emotional development.

Alternative Theories

Since Maslow's Hierarchy of Needs, others have proposed alternative views.

Manfred Max-Neef was a Chilean economist who rejected the notion of a hierarchy and instead suggested that the fundamental needs of humans are interrelated:

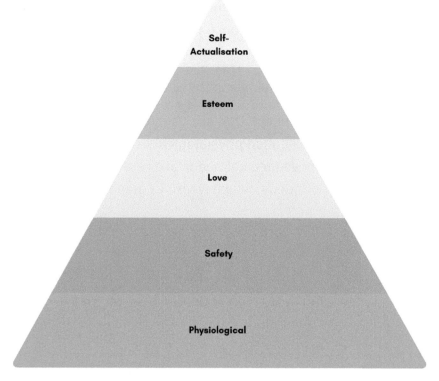

FIGURE 2.1. Graphic showing Maslow's Hierarchy

- Subsistence
- Protection
- Affection
- Understanding
- Participation
- Leisure
- Creation
- Identity
- Freedom.

William Glasser was an American psychiatrist who proposed a model that was similar to Maslow's but was less developmental and more dynamic in its nature. His 'Choice Theory' explains that humans' behaviour and choices are influenced by their desire to satisfy the following five needs:

- Survival
- Love and Belonging
- Power
- Freedom
- Fun.

Educator's View – Jim Hoerricks, PhD (non-verbal autistic advocate, researcher, author, lecturer and educator)

Glasser's Choice Theory, the theory that we are always seeking to satisfy one or more of five basic human needs, explains why we autistics choose to do what we do better than any other theoretical construct. Many of us need to wander, to explore. We seemingly ignore safety needs (there goes Maslow). We seemingly care not for esteem and affection. We care so deeply to explore (or roam) the world in the peace of solitude. Perhaps this is related to our sensory issues – the often-overwhelming noise that bombards us in crowded places.

It's important to note here that every autistic person is different in their sensory-seeking/avoiding aspects. For example, some sensory seekers ignore safety needs and taste or eat things that are dangerous. On the other hand, some sensory avoiders wouldn't consider leaving their houses and must be convinced to venture out. Again, autism is a spectrum. But we can use Choice Theory to help make sense of what an autistic person is doing at a given point – e.g., what need(s) are they attempting to satisfy.

When examined through the lens of Glasser's Choice Theory and Basic Needs, autistic behaviour makes perfect sense. We have the basic need to matter, make a difference, achieve, be competent, recognised, and respected (Power). We also have the basic need for agency, for making our own choices, being independent and autonomous (Freedom). Freedom is about being able to move freely without restriction. Glasser's theory notes that our Basic Needs don't really change over time and that our attempts to satisfy them happen unconsciously.

(Adapted from Hoerricks 2023)

There have been a range of other theorists who have suggested alternative models on the same theme. For the remainder of this chapter, we will focus on four aspects taken from these models that feel most appropriate for our work in the early years.

Physiological Needs

In our early years setting or school, we may well be in a position to quickly identify if a child is lacking in any of the physiological factors. For children who are confident, verbal communicators, they are likely to tell us if they are feeling hungry, thirsty, tired or cold. With very young children and babies, we tend to use a process of elimination. Alternatively, for children who are able to move independently, they may seek to satisfy their needs by heading to the snack cupboard or taking themselves to the reading area for a lie down. If these things are happening on a regular basis and patterns are emerging, it is important to follow up and seek an understanding as to why their basic physiological needs are not being met. For children with complex support needs, it can be harder to identify if a child is lacking in one of these areas. In these circumstances, it is imperative that we endeavour to form high-quality bonds with children so that we can notice if something isn't right. A child with complex physical and medical support needs may, for example, suggest discomfort or unhappiness in subtle ways that can only be interpreted accurately by a close and trusted person.

In any of these circumstances, the next steps for an educator after identifying a deficiency in one or more of the basic physiological needs can be challenging. Scenarios such as this are made less difficult if we have already sought to establish high-quality relationships with the families of the children in our care (see Chapter

11). It is essential that we handle conversations with family members in a sensitive manner, with compassion at the forefront of our minds. When we fear a child is being neglected, it may be that our first emotion is frustration or anger. We must strive for understanding and empathy first and foremost. Our aim is to improve the situation, not create additional barriers between home and the setting/school. The family of the child may well be very grateful that you have raised your concerns, as it could be something they have been struggling with at home.

Once your concern has been communicated and discussed, it is important that you aim to work together with the family, and, if necessary, health professionals, to improve the situation. Is there anything you can do or ideas that you have that could better the situation? It might be that you can support in trying a variety of cups/bottles for a child who is reluctant to take in fluids. It could be adding flexibility to your routines to allow a nap for a child during the day. Regardless of the strategies, the key aspect is that you work closely with the family to seek a solution.

Obviously, if there is ever a safeguarding concern, the appropriate procedures should be followed. In these circumstances too, good relationships and communication with a child's family is important.

Safety Needs

What makes us feel safe can be very personal and individual. Having appropriate physical shelter is certainly a significant factor in our safety, but we can't make too many presumptions about the recipe for a feeling of safety for an individual. It might be that for one child a very structured, calm and predictable routine allows them to build trust in their early years provision. For another, freedom to go with the flow and respond in the moment provides a feeling of safety and contentment, even if for others this might feel too chaotic. In almost all cases, however, young children need to know and to trust the adults in an educational environment, especially those working closest to them. It is their guidance, and ability to comfort and reassure when things don't go so well that can contribute hugely to a sense of safety.

Although it might not be straightforward to identify the exact ingredients for an individual's feelings of safety, it should be easier to recognise if they are beginning to feel unsafe. When we feel unsafe or unhappy, we usually respond with a level of anxiety, which may manifest itself in a range of ways. It could be that a child is showing a lack of engagement or is withdrawing from social situations. They may appear scared, or become visibly upset. Whatever the presentation, it is hugely important that we attempt to address the issues as quickly as possible. An autistic child, for instance, may be experiencing a level of distress due to sensory sensitivities (see Chapter 9). A child with a physical disability may feel unable to keep themselves safe if children around them are being very boisterous. If a child feels unsafe, there is a very low chance that they will be able to fully engage with a learning environment – adjustments must be made ASAP. The actions that educators take to help a child feel safer contribute significantly to the level of trust they will receive from a child in the future. Establishing trusting relationships with the children in our group should be one of our highest priorities.

Love and Belonging Needs

We have a crucial role as educators in identifying if we have concerns that a child may be suffering from neglect. It may not be immediately obvious, particularly if a child feels happy and safe at nursery/school, but if we do become aware that a child is lacking love, care and affection at home, we must follow the safeguarding procedures as laid out by the relevant policies. The need for love and belonging isn't, however, exclusive to home life.

In her 2018 paper 'Characterising the principles of Professional Love in early childhood care and education', Jools Page coined the term 'Professional Love' in relation to the bonds that form between young children and their professional primary caregivers. Understandably, over recent years there has been a reluctance to provide physical contact or comfort to a child in a setting or school, for fear that accusations of inappropriateness may be made. It is so important, however, to consider the importance of caregiving in our role as educators in the early years.

> Professional Love, as I have characterised it, does not attempt to apply a universal definition of love [or intimacy or care], into a criteria checklist. Rather, it provides an opportunity for critical reflection and adaptation which takes account of these fleeting, yet crucial exchanges which occur between young children and their professional primary caregivers. Thus, each setting can generate its own phenomenology of Professional Love. In practical terms this should lead to the creation of policies and procedures which give confidence to caregivers about cuddling young children without fear of reprisal.
>
> *(Page, 2018, p.15)*

As Jools mentions, it would be helpful to have a policy in your setting or school which acknowledges the importance of providing appropriate physical and emotional support to the children in your care. I previously worked in a school that had a 'Positive Touch' policy which outlined the reasons why physical contact was important and necessary but also set out expectations as to what this looked like and how staff members could ensure they kept both the children and themselves safe. Self-reflection is again the key to contemplating how best to harbour a feeling of belonging in our setting or school. What unique factors contribute to our own feeling of belonging? Is it the people we are with? Or the familiarity of an area or environment? Is it a knowledge that the people around us have our best interests at heart? Or does it link to our safety as previously discussed?

The likelihood is that it is a combination of these factors, as well as many more. Whatever the individual factors, it is our role to ensure where possible that all our children have the opportunity to experience this feeling. The starting point to facilitate this must be actively seeking to get to know the children in our group on a deeper level. Figure 2.2 suggests what deeper understanding of a child might look like. It is important to note that it is not a good idea to try to ascertain this information in an impersonal or clinical manner. A parent may feel there is a risk of judgement or a level of intrusion if faced with a questionnaire or an interview during a home visit. This information will become available more naturally if efforts are made to establish genuine connections with families of the children in your care.

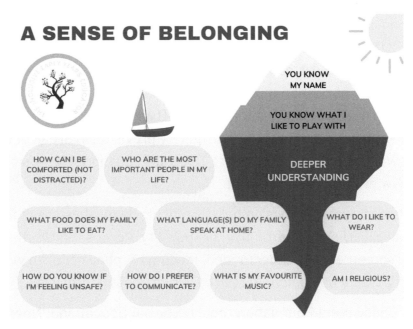

FIGURE 2.2 Graphic showing what deeper understanding of a child might look like

Freedom and Fun

More often than not, we are in the privileged position in the early years to be able to design our provision and environment in a way that will be as motivating and engaging as possible for our children. Unfortunately, as children make their way through the subsequent stages of school, educators aren't necessarily in a position to enable learning in a way that provides autonomy to the learner. This is as good a reason as any to ensure that we resist the temptation to overly formalise our teaching practices for our children in the EYFS.

Back to self-reflection, we are acutely aware that we are much more likely to engage in learning when:

- we are interested in the subject matter
- the subject matter is presented in an engaging way
- we can make choices about the direction we want to take our learning in
- we are having fun.

In my opinion, these reflection points are very relevant to the teaching of children at any stage of education. When reviewing the quality of provision, the first question I ask myself is 'Are the children truly engaged?' This is a useful starting point when considering how well children are progressing in our setting or school.

Reflecting on Basic Needs in Doncaster

The link between deprivation and SEND was an essential consideration when designing the Reflection Toolkit. The percentage of pupils entitled to pupil premium in Doncaster primary schools is above the national average: 31.6 per cent in Doncaster in comparison to 26.9 per cent nationally (based on the Census data, January 2023). The overlap between deprivation and SEND is no secret, particularly when considering the access and impact of high-quality provision in areas of deprivation. The Joseph Rowntree Foundation's report 'Special Educational Needs and their link to poverty' (Shaw et al., 2016) noted that:

> High-quality early years provision has a particularly positive effect for both children with SEND and children living in poverty. Across the UK, the early years system is fragmented and underfunded, leading to many children with SEND who are living in poverty being unable to access high-quality provision.

The Education Endowment Foundation report 'Special Educational Needs in Mainstream Schools: Five recommendations on special education needs in mainstream schools' also highlighted that pupils with SEND are twice as likely to be eligible for free school meals.

The area Doncaster Local Authority serves is a mixed locality with many pockets of deprivation and affluence. The landscape is also unique with large areas of rural farming land mixed with inner-city high-rise housing. Each area has its own individual identity due to the makeup of the community it serves. The current Index of Multiple Deprivation (IMD) statistics (2019) show that Doncaster and Barnsley are equal as the most deprived LAs in South Yorkshire, closely followed by Rotherham and then Sheffield, all of whom perform worse than the national average.

Like many areas of the UK, families in Doncaster are currently experiencing extraordinary daily challenges, due to the cost-of-living crisis and the aftermath of a global pandemic which has had a lasting impact. One striking aspect about early years educators in Doncaster is their commitment to improving outcomes for children.

Educators I talk to every day are passionate about helping and supporting the families they work with. It's uplifting to work with so many individuals who are open-minded about the ways they can make a real difference to children's lives. Pennie Akehurst from Early Years Fundamentals works frequently in partnership with the Doncaster Local Authority. Pennie spoke recently at a celebration event for early years providers about their courage and determination in what had been the most challenging few years in our sector's history.

Stephanie Douglas, previous Head of Service for Early Years, Intervention and Prevention at Doncaster Council was awarded the MBE for services to Education and Early Years in 2021. Recognised for her leadership and support to Doncaster early years settings during the Covid pandemic, Steph helped early years providers to remain open to support children of key workers and vulnerable children. Steph describes her ethos and the nature of early years providers during the pandemic:

> During the Covid pandemic early years educators in Doncaster went above and beyond to support young children and families. Many showed determination to continue to stay open while implementing challenging restrictions and adapted their settings to continue to provide rich learning experiences. I am honoured to have worked alongside Doncaster early years educators in schools, nurseries, playgroups and childminders and local authority support services.
>
> My passion is making a difference to young children. I think that the earlier you provide intervention for families in need, the more successful children will be

when they become adults. It's a wonderful job working alongside educators with the same ethos in Doncaster and working with young children is the most rewarding thing in the world.

Steph Douglas (former Head of Service for Intervention and
Prevention at Doncaster Council)

Reflecting on Psychological Needs – A Case Study

A few weeks before the Covid pandemic hit, I attended a training programme in Doncaster run by Brenda Cheer, Specialist Continence Nurse for ERIC (The Children's Bowel and Bladder Charity). My colleague Shelley Petta (Early Years Inclusion Officer – Lead for Assessment) had organised for Brenda to deliver the training programme to a range of partners in Health, Early Years and Family Hubs with the aim of training a team of practitioners who could support children and parents with toilet training.

Over the last few years in Doncaster, we have seen a growing number of settings and schools requesting support for toileting. Settings report that there has been an increase in children toilet training later, with one school reporting that up to 40 per cent of the Foundation 1 cohort in 2018/2019 were not toilet trained. Also, Doncaster's percentage of children achieving their Early Learning Goal in Managing Self has gradually decreased over the last few years (89.2% in 2019, 86.5% in 2022, 85% in 2023). Many schools found that decreased toileting skills had led to a drop in the percentage of children achieving the ELG in this area. This was identified as an area of concern for our team.

I have supported many families over decades with toileting, but the training from ERIC was new to me and offered a completely different approach to planning and preparation for toilet training, and it focused mainly on the physiology of the individual child. This knowledge and understanding was invaluable and has informed much of my work with settings and schools when considering aspects of toileting, but has also prompted reflective thinking about the importance of ensuring physiological needs are met and how these needs can impact on many other areas of development.

A school in the east of Doncaster contacted me in summer 2020 regarding Daisy who attended their setting. Daisy had previously accessed support from the Portage Service. The school described having difficulties managing Daisy's toileting needs and reported that she was having a number of accidents each day. Although Mum felt that Daisy was mostly dry and toilet trained at home, they were having so many accidents in school that the teaching staff had suggested going back to wearing a pull-up in school as changing was becoming unmanageable. Mum was understandably resistant to putting Daisy back in nappies. Mum felt this was a step back and couldn't understand why toileting in school was so different from home for her child.

I attended a meeting with the school and parents, using the Reflection Toolkit to support a discussion on physiological needs. I gave advice and recommendations based upon the ERIC model of toileting, the first step being to track the intake and output of the child's bowel and bladder movements to be able to find out more about the child's physiology. This model focuses on finding out about and promoting the need for children to have a healthy bowel and bladder; identifying aspects such as constipation can be particularly important in how successful toileting develops.

Parents and the school completed ERIC's Intake/Output Chart over a period of a few days to check whether Daisy displayed signs of a healthy bladder and bowel. This is identified by the drink and food the child consumes (the intake) and the frequency, consistency and volume of the wees and poos the child expels (the output). I asked the school and parents to check whether Daisy was showing signs of a healthy bladder, as recommended by ERIC – i.e. drinking 6–8 glasses of fluid (preferably water, but water-based drinks and milk are OK too) per day and able to hold their wee for one to one and a half hours, with bowel movements being anything from three times a day to three or four times a week (pooing at least every other day) and a consistency which should be soft, sausage shaped and easy to pass.

When signs of a healthy bowel and bladder were observed, I then advised developing a toileting plan in school focusing on enabling Daisy to have the most chance of success. This involved taking Daisy to the toilet every one to one and a half hours and also encouraging her to sit on the toilet 20–30 minutes after food, as recommended by ERIC.

I gave the school advice and information from the ERIC website and we reflected on the information gained from the intake/output chart. We identified that the school was currently taking Daisy to the toilet *before* eating, rather than 20 minutes *after* a meal – the optimal time for success. They also observed Daisy was drinking very little at school, resulting in her being unable to exercise her bladder. This meant she had a reduced feeling of her bladder being full, which affected her success at being able to wee when taken to the toilet.

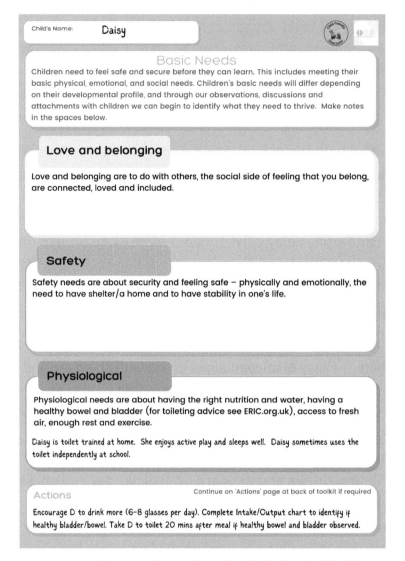

FIGURE 2.3 An example page from Daisy's Reflection Toolkit

Based upon their reflections, the school changed their approach to toileting, and this resulted in success for Daisy. Within three weeks of the new approach, Daisy was rarely having any wetting accidents at school. Figure 2.3 shows how the school completed the Basic Needs page in the Reflection Toolkit.

As an ERIC Nurse, I deliver a lot of teaching, to health care professionals and early years practitioners. Whether I'm focusing on toilet training an autistic child, night-time wetting or a complex bladder condition, I always start with the fundamentals – how do the bladder and bowel actually work? The tendency is to focus on what comes out and where it goes, rather than how it was made, stored and evacuated. But that insight makes it so much easier to understand why things sometimes go wrong – and subsequently how to put things right. Time and again, I have seen 'the penny drop' as the practitioner realises that a child's apparent behaviour is driven by what's going on in their bladder and/or bowel.

I believe that every professional working with children needs to receive training on healthy bladders and bowels and toilet training – it could be from ERIC or from a local provider. It should, of course, be part of the fundamental training for any role caring for children – hopefully, one day it will be!

But why is it so important? What is the effect of poor bladder and bowel health and poor toileting on the child? Let me give you a couple of examples:

- Constipation in childhood is very common – one in three children will experience it, with the highest prevalence among toddlers. Symptoms can include pain, nausea, soiling (i.e. leaking poo into pants), frequent, small wees with possible wetting, as well as more general symptoms like headache, lethargy and irritability. Would you be able to focus on learning if you had tummy ache and were feeling sick? How would you feel if you kept having poo and/or wee accidents? Low self-esteem is a barrier to learning, as well as hindering social interaction. But constipation is easy to treat, with laxatives as the first line in accordance with NICE Guidelines. Wouldn't it be good if all early years practitioners could not only recognise the signs and symptoms of constipation but signpost to family-friendly information and advise of the need to see the GP for laxatives.
- Children with a learning disability are often late to toilet train. But do they need to be? It is the health of the bladder and bowel that determines readiness for toilet training – not the child's ability to communicate their need for the toilet, or them having the motor skills to allow independence with clothing, etc. Many neurodivergent children will never show any signs of awareness of needing a wee or poo, but that doesn't stop them getting it in the toilet!

The longer the child wears a nappy or pull-up, the harder it will be for them to master toileting – why make it more difficult for them? The bladder and bowel are not disabled...

Starting nursery or school is a huge milestone for any child and can be more of a challenge for a child with a disability. Let's increase their independence by not leaving them in a nappy.

Brenda Cheer (Specialist Continence Nurse for ERIC)

FIGURE 2.4 A QR code linking to the ERIC website

You can find more information and resources at the ERIC website by scanning Figure 2.4.

Advocating for a healthy bowel and bladder in Doncaster has continued to be a focus for training. With increasing numbers of children being trained later, we also offer bespoke training to settings who want to enable change. The training promotes much of the ERIC advice and resources, and also encourages reflection of toileting environments in early years settings, the timing of when educators speak to parents about toileting and how to prompt conversations about healthy bowels and bladders through areas of provision (e.g. domestic play and book corner).

Louise Hobbs (EYFS Leader) at Bentley New Village Primary School, a school with high levels of deprivation and increasing SEND needs, describes the changes they made following reflection on physiological needs.

Louise and her team attended at a 'Wee and Poo – Promoting Healthy Bladders and Bowels' training session. The number of children entering nursery at Bentley New Village Primary School has more than doubled in recent years. Struggling with low levels of parent engagement, Louise and the early years team have made a number of significant changes to improve outcomes for children in this area.

After attending the 'Wee and Poo' training delivered by Ann Lowe, my colleagues and I decided to input changes into our practice. We initiated open and honest conversations with our parents about their barriers to toilet training. We quickly discovered that, with the majority of cases, the parents were saying because the children were non-speaking or had communication differences, they weren't able to communicate when they needed the toilet. We worked closely with our parents and gave them factual information from the training about the physiology of the body during toilet training. We asked them to keep a wee/poo diary to track when the children were wetting/soiling. We also suggested to some parents that their child may need to visit a GP as they may be suffering with constipation. The parents were able to communicate to us how many times their children wet/ soil in a day, how much they drink and for how long they can hold their wee. This showed us that they had read and understood the information we provided for them.

We also spent time ensuring our toilet area was an inviting space for the children. We lowered the ceilings, painted the walls and decorated it in a jungle theme. We have music playing and a diffuser with calming scents in order to make the toileting experience more friendly.

In June 2023, we had 12 children visit us for our stay and play session who were not yet toilet trained. After working with these parents over the holidays and prior to them starting school, we had reduced this number to eight children when they arrived in September.

We continued to have regular meetings with parents and send them information and links to the ERIC website for support, and in November 2023 we had only four children not fully trained.

As a school, we are thrilled with the progress that has been made in this area in such a short space of time due to the training and support given by Ann Lowe and the ERIC charity.

Louise Hobbs (EYFS Leader at Bentley New Village Primary School)

Reflecting on Safety Needs – A Case Study

The importance of a home, shelter and a place to sleep resonated with me in a recent visit to a school in the north of Doncaster. The Reflection Toolkit helped to highlight the impact of this basic need on children's learning.

Kian was a little boy who accessed nursery provision at his local school. The school had identified Kian's support needs early in the first term of his nursery year. Kian communicated using single words; he became frustrated when he struggled to communicate his needs and would show strong emotional responses to transitions, such as coming inside from outside. Kian benefited from using strategies such as objects of reference and visual prompts to help him understand when things were going to happen.

The school had a good relationship with Kian's family, and they had visited the family home prior to Kian starting at the school. Kian had good relationships with his family and strong attachments to his parents and sibling at home, but the physical environment of his home was more challenging. Kian's family had experienced a range of difficulties with their rented house and maintenance of the building. There were concerns from Kian's parents about the suitability of the property and aspects of safety. This eventually resulted in his family leaving the property and being rehoused in a nearby hostel while they waited for another property to become available. The hostel was a different environment from where Kian had previously lived, and the family were living together in one room to rest, sleep, eat and socialise.

The educators at the setting observed that during the time of moving to and living at the hostel, Kian had begun to show less engagement and more dysregulated behaviours, and he appeared more unsettled in nursery. The SENCO and class teacher met with Kian's mother to discuss support and next steps for Kian and the family. They shared their observations and the changes they had noticed in his behaviour and engagement. Kian's mum explained that the time in the hostel had been difficult for all the family. There were loud noises that kept her up for much of the night, and the children didn't sleep easily. Mum said that Kian was unable to get to sleep, and he seemed agitated and unsettled. Kian's mum wondered whether he felt safe in the environment. As we explored his feelings at the meeting, Kian's mother shared that there seemed to be an increase in the number of times he would cry and become upset at the hostel, and it was difficult to reassure him so that he could rest and sleep. Mum also said that he frequently woke in the night, which was not uncommon in their previous house but had increased significantly.

We reflected on the impact of this change for Kian, as a collective group, and planned for adaptations in provision to increase Kian's sense of safety and belonging in the nursery, using the Reflection Toolkit (see Figure 2.5).

With the adjustments to their provision for Kian in place, educators at the setting observed that Kian began to demonstrate more regulated behaviours and settled better into nursery. Having consideration of these aspects and their impact on Kian's learning was integral to improving his engagement in learning and supporting his development.

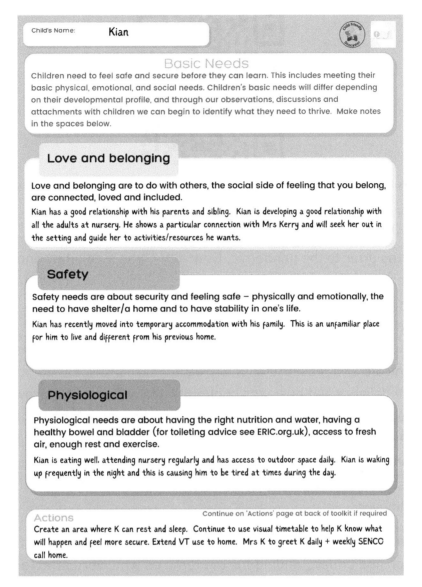

FIGURE 2.5 An example page from Kian's Reflection Toolkit

Sindy Hinchliffe, Leanne Webster (Portage Home Visitors) and Bev Downes (Area SENCO) are all Sleep Trained Practitioners who give advice and strategies to parents and early years providers about the importance of sleep and rest. At a recent CPD afternoon, they advocated for the importance of sleep as a vital component of health and wellbeing. They shared that a range of medical conditions such as Reflux, Asthma, Eczema, Epilepsy and/or neurodivergence such as Autism and ADHD can cause sleep disturbance. Aspects such as routine, sleepy foods, clothing and bath time are all important to reflect on to enable children (and adults) to get the best night's sleep. Further information from The Sleep Charity is available by scanning Figure 2.6.

FIGURE 2.6 A QR code linking to The Sleep Charity's Useful Resources page

Reflecting on Love and Belonging– A Case Study

In the few months prior to the pandemic, Doncaster was also hit by another devastating event – flooding. In November 2019, riverbanks in Doncaster burst and villages to the east of the city were impacted hugely by flood water. Early years settings responded in remarkable ways to best serve the communities. As an early years service, we too went into a critical response phase. Our first phase of response was to communicate and reassure as many early years providers as possible about funding, service delivery and business continuity. Many Doncaster providers had already actioned their plans and made adjustments to support the families affected, offering adjusted hours, different sessions and food and shelter to families who couldn't return to their homes. The aftermath of the flooding resulted in a number of families accessing temporary accommodation for a period of time until they rebuilt their homes and lives.

I spoke to a range of providers during this difficult period, all of whom acted with compassion and understanding for the families who were affected. I spoke frequently to one particular childminder, over the period of a few weeks. The childminding setting had been affected by flooding; their garden was still under water but they had managed to return to their home. What struck me was that the childminder had little concern for her own situation. Her main concern was for the children who came to her setting, including one family who had suffered the devastating impact of losing their home and many of their belongings. The childminder contacted us seeking advice on whether she had information about every service possible to support the family. Asking questions such as: Where is the nearest food bank? What bedding, clothing and funding are available for families? Could she offer additional hours out of her usual working day? Could the funding be stretched to enable the child to access the setting during school holidays and at different times?

It was an emotional experience for the childminder; she could see parents struggling to come to terms with the situation they found themselves in. The childminder noticed that the mother of the family was worried, anxious and upset about their circumstances and what they needed to do next. She also observed that the child had become more clingy to parents at drop-off and that it often took more time to settle them when they came to the setting. They would be upset for a period of time, and this would have a knock-on effect on the other children who came to the setting.

The childminder discussed her worries with me, and, reflecting on the child's basic needs, we agreed on strategies to try to support the child to be more settled when entering the setting. The childminder had also observed that these changes in the child's behaviour had created increased anxiety for the parents who had a lot on their plate and were finding their child's unsettledness challenging and difficult to manage. We discussed strategies such as using areas of interest to support the child to settle more quickly.

The childminder had observed that the child had a particular interest in trains and vehicles. She planned to set up a small world vehicle area in the lounge ready for when the child was dropped off. It was decided that adapting the usual drop-off procedure (at the door) would be beneficial and instead planned to encourage the parent to come into the setting and drop off in the lounge, where the child would hopefully be absorbed and engaged in their area of interest before the parent left.

We also looked at adjusting the arrival time for the child, so the parent could drop off ten minutes earlier. This would give the parent more time to settle their child, before being joined by the rest of the group. We thought about how to communicate these possible changes to the parent, and agreed that drop-off and pick-up times were not ideal for conversations; the child would become increasingly distressed having to wait while the childminder and the parent discussed the situation. We felt that it would be best to contact the parent and discuss a plan over the phone at a mutually convenient time. The changes worked really well, and over the next few weeks, the child became more settled and happier in the setting, showing much greater levels of wellbeing and engagement, enabling deeper learning and involvement to take place.

Figure 2.7 (p. 44) shows the notes the childminder made in the child's Reflection Toolkit.

Reflecting on Freedom and Fun – A Case Study

Having taught throughout the primary age range myself, one of the aspects that draws me to early years and keeps me there is the freedom early years offers for us

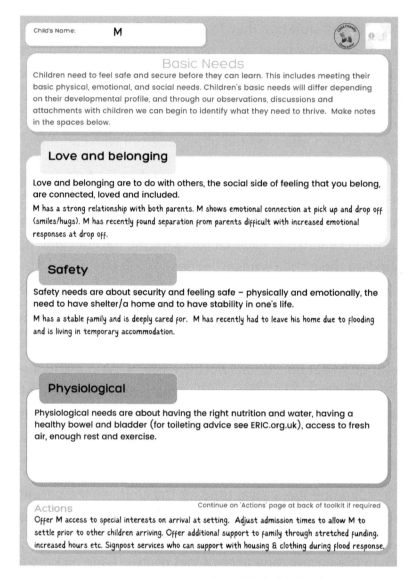

FIGURE 2.7 An example page from M's Reflection Toolkit

to take learning in any direction. As a colleague once said to me about early years, 'Our only ceiling is the sky.' I find myself having countless conversations with early years settings in Doncaster about how lucky we are in early years to be able to engage children in motivating experiences that focus on an individual child's joy in learning.

In schools, I love to invite junior colleagues into the early years world. In a recent experience, a new SENCO (also a Key Stage 2 teacher) from a feeder school came to visit an early years setting to observe a group of children who were transitioning to their Reception class. It was interesting to see her responses as children highly engaged in the outside mud kitchen and potion station brought her mud pies and cocktails to enjoy. I could see the teacher was quite out of her comfort zone at first, but as we discussed the children, she observed and commented that communication, negotiation, fine motor and social skills were developing at a rate of knots, due to the children being so highly engaged in the resources on offer.

Next on the agenda for the morning was the sprinkler in the outside area – something the visiting SENCO wasn't prepared for and couldn't really understand the importance of children accessing at first. Charlie, one of the children in the group who was transitioning to school, was particularly motivated by the water sprinkler. He found such joy in moving in and out of the spray, and he loved the feeling of water falling on his body and face. He used buckets and bottles to collect the water and pour it into guttering tubes and cups. His communication skills in water-based activities were at the optimum level and his babble in the sprinkler was melodic, tuneful and exciting to hear. You could almost hear the cogs whirring in his brain the moment the sprinkler went on.

I spoke to the SENCO about his journey to this point, how we had found it difficult to work out what helped him to regulate in the beginning and that it had been difficult to settle him at times. When the SENCO had observed him accessing the sprinkler, she could see the engagement and the enjoyment he felt, so much so that she wanted to get under the sprinkler herself and experience the same joy. The first thing on the list to support transition was a hosepipe and sprinkler! It had even led to reflection on enjoyment for her Key Stage 2 class and she considered planning an afternoon of water play with them. It was a thought-provoking discussion about the importance of freedom and fun being so vital for learning for all children (and adults)!

Thought Provocations

- Do you have an awareness of whether children's basic needs are being met in your setting/school?
- Are your relationships with families strong enough to discuss potentially challenging topics around a child's basic needs?

References

Education Endowment Foundation (2021) *Special Educational Needs in Mainstream Schools: Creating a Positive Learning Environment for Pupils with SEN.* Lived Places Publishing. https://livedplacespublishing.com/book/isbn/9781915271822

Hoerricks, J. (2023) No Place for Autism? Lived Places Publishing. https://livedplacespublishing.com/book/isbn/9781915271822

Lieberman, M.D. (2015) *Social: Why Our Brains Are Wired to Connect*. Oxford University Press.

Maslow, A.H. (1943) A theory of human motivation. *Psychological Review 50*(4), 370–396. https://psycnet.apa.org/doi/10.1037/h0054346

Ministry of Housing, Communities and Local Government (2019) Index of Multiple Deprivation. www.gov.uk/government/statistics/english-indices-of-deprivation-2019

Page, J. (2018) Characterising the principles of Professional Love in early childhood care and education. *International Journal of Early Years Education 26*(2), 125–141. https://doi.org/10.1080/09669760.2018.1459508

Shaw, B., Bernardes, E., Trethewey, A. and Menzies, L. (2016) Special educational needs and their links to poverty. Joseph Rowntree Foundation. www.jrf.org.uk/report/special-educational-needs-and-their-links-poverty

Child's Name

Basic Needs

Children need to feel safe and secure before they can learn. This includes meeting their basic physical, emotional and social needs. Children's basic needs will differ depending on their developmental profile, and through our observations, discussions and attachments with children, we can begin to identify what they need to thrive. Make notes in the spaces below.

Love and Belonging

Love and belonging are to do with others, the social side of feeling that you belong, are connected, loved and included.

Actions

Copyright material from Ann Lowe and Stephen Kilgour (2025), *The Inclusive Early Years Educator*, Routledge

Child's Name

Basic Needs

Children need to feel safe and secure before they can learn. This includes meeting their basic physical, emotional and social needs. Children's basic needs will differ depending on their developmental profile, and through our observations, discussions and attachments with children, we can begin to identify what they need to thrive. Make notes in the spaces below.

Safety

Safety needs are about security and feeling safe – physically and emotionally, the need to have shelter/a home and to have stability in one's life.

Actions

Copyright material from Ann Lowe and Stephen Kilgour (2025), *The Inclusive Early Years Educator*, Routledge

Child's Name

Basic Needs

Children need to feel safe and secure before they can learn. This includes meeting their basic physical, emotional and social needs. Children's basic needs will differ depending on their developmental profile, and through our observations, discussions and attachments with children, we can begin to identify what they need to thrive. Make notes in the spaces below.

Physiological

Physiological needs are about having the right nutrition and water, having a healthy bowel and bladder (for toileting advice, see ERIC.org.uk), access to fresh air, enough rest and exercise.

Actions

Copyright material from Ann Lowe and Stephen Kilgour (2025), *The Inclusive Early Years Educator*, Routledge

Child's Name

Basic Needs

Children need to feel safe and secure before they can learn. This includes meeting their basic physical, emotional and social needs. Children's basic needs will differ depending on their developmental profile, and through our observations, discussions and attachments with children, we can begin to identify what they need to thrive. Make notes in the spaces below.

Freedom and Fun

Freedom allows us to make choices and have control over our learning to make plans and decide on our own next steps. Fun relates to our need to find joy and satisfaction while we learn.

Actions

Copyright material from Ann Lowe and Stephen Kilgour (2025), *The Inclusive Early Years Educator*, Routledge

Chapter 3

WELLBEING AND INVOLVEMENT

What Is Wellbeing?

In its most straightforward form, we can literally describe wellbeing as 'being well' – whether that be physically or mentally. Perhaps an even simpler definition would be 'happy and healthy'. The increased focus on wellbeing, particularly regarding mental health, has generally been welcomed in both education and society as a whole. The fact that high-profile celebrities and sportspeople are increasingly talking openly about their own struggles with mental health means that conversations about our own wellbeing feel more normalised, although still extremely challenging.

To feel happy and healthy is a very individual experience. As much as the obvious benefits of living a healthy lifestyle can contribute to a higher sense of mental wellbeing, this isn't an exact science, not a one-size-fits-all. Many people may not be aware of what it is that will provide them with the feeling of happiness they crave, or why their own pursuit of happiness isn't necessarily following the path required to reach it – often through no fault of their own.

Reflecting on what contributes to a sense of feeling well for ourselves is a sensible starting point before considering the wellbeing of others in our care. The old adage 'Put your own life jacket on first' is certainly appropriate when working with young children. The fact that our lives are often made up of distinct areas means that this is unlikely to be a quick exercise. We might have a family life, a work life and a social life to consider (in no particular order). What makes us feel energised and well in our home environment may not match the criteria that we contemplate in our working life. Finding balance between the various aspects of our being is usually beneficial – and when we reflect on times of stress and anxiety, at least one area of our life is likely to have been causing us higher levels of strain than desired.

It is also important to take into consideration that a good level of emotional wellbeing may look different for different people – particularly for people with learning differences. As we are all unique, the signs of contentment may contrast significantly from one person to another. In addition, on a given day, our route to achieving the optimum level of wellbeing may also vary hugely.

> If we are better trained to understand factors that influence our mental health and better equipped to address issues when they arise, we can learn to take proactive steps to prevent and reduce job stressors, which has the potential to enhance the wellbeing of the whole community."
>
> *(Moxley, 2023, p.7)*

What Is Involvement?

An alternative word that is often used in education is 'engagement'. It is fairly common knowledge that the more involved or engaged we are in learning, the more effective the process will be. Unfortunately for our colleagues in subsequent stages of education, the remit for designing child-centred, truly engaging provision is restricted by more formal approaches. Thankfully, in the early years there is often greater licence to create learning environments that inspire awe and wonder.

Another word that is intrinsically linked to involvement is 'concentration'. Especially in the technological age in which we live, moments of pure concentration and involvement can be harder to find than in days of old. There are so many potential distractions – provided mostly by our favourite hand-held electronic device. Even in our most significant moments of joy, we can often lose sight of the moment through our desire to capture the event on our phone (also a very relevant point when it comes to capturing moments of learning in the EYFS – balance is everything).

The Leuven Scale

The Leuven Scale is a tool that was developed by a team from the Research Centre for Experiential Education (Leuven University, Belgium), supervised by Dr Ferre Laevers. The resource contains two five-point scales to measure Wellbeing (Table 3.1) and Involvement (Table 3.2).

Criticisms of the Leuven Scale

It can be argued that the Leuven Scale isn't as effective or appropriate when used with neurodivergent children. For example, the descriptions of the levels for both involvement and wellbeing don't take into account that an autistic child might show involvement in different ways to a neurotypical peer. The same could also be said for

TABLE 3.1 The Scale for Wellbeing

Level	Wellbeing	Signals
1	Extremely low	The child clearly shows signals of discomfort.
2	Low	The posture, facial expression and actions indicate that the child does not feel at ease.
3	Moderate	The child has a neutral posture. Facial expression and posture show little or no emotion.
4	High	The child shows obvious signs of satisfaction; however, these signals are not constantly present with the same intensity as in Level 5.
5	Extremely high	The child looks happy and cheerful, smiles, is spontaneous, expressive and relaxed. They are lively, full of energy and express self-confidence and self-assurance.

Source: Laevers, 2005

TABLE 3.2 The Scale for Involvement

Level	Involvement	Signals
1	Extremely low	The child hardly shows any activity.
2	Low	The child shows some degree of activity, but it is often interrupted.
3	Moderate	The child is busy the whole time, but without real concentration.
4.	High	There are clear signs of involvement, but these are not always present to their full extent.
5	Extremely high	The child is continuously engaged in the activity and completely absorbed in it.

Source: Laevers, 2005

the signals of wellbeing for a child from a different culture. Invariably in our society, we look for signs of pleasure and enjoyment as a key indicator of happiness. In other cultures, the focus is often on achieving happiness through experiences of meaning and purpose. It is unrealistic that these tools in their current form could provide genuinely useful information across a varied cohort of children. Like any resource that is suggested in education, we must determine whether it is appropriate for some, most or all the children in our care.

Tuning In

Spending time observing children closely and learning about their engagement levels is important. But we must also make time to 'tune in' to each individual child in an effort to better understand how they feel motivated – and in turn support their levels of wellbeing and involvement.

I previously created Figure 3.1 to support educators when meeting children for the first time – sometimes keeping things simple is the best way when it comes to working with young children.

FIGURE 3.1 Tips for tuning in

The Child's View

As well as using observational tools and techniques to 'tune in' to a child to support our understanding of their levels of wellbeing and involvement, we must also remember to seek the actual thoughts of each child. It might be that a child is able to verbally communicate how engaging they are finding a particular activity, or how they are feeling. For those who communicate in different (just as important) ways, we must facilitate opportunities for them to share their views. This might be providing a chat/response board with pictures/symbols to support understanding, or it could be that we learn to better understand a child's gestures and choice making to ensure that we 'hear' their voice. For more on this topic, see Chapter 10.

Educator's View – Abi Miranda, Head of Early Years and Prevention, Anna Freud

Wellbeing is such an important but under-recognised topic in education and care. We often fail to notice its presence, but the absence of wellbeing has a huge impact on children and the workforce. It is important to consider the part that involvement plays in wellbeing.

There is a continuum between feeling that things are done to us and how much we feel we can influence our circumstances. Recognising that we can intentionally maintain and improve our circumstances is known as personal agency. We know from mental health research that having a sense of agency in your own life is linked to better outcomes. It is important to recognise that people from under-heard communities are likelier to have had experiences where their views seemed not to matter, which can decrease our sense of personal agency.

As practitioners, we must also reflect on our own sense of involvement and agency. We work within pre-determined frameworks and routines, but within that, we must retain our own sense of independence and creativity, so we are using our professional judgement to support the wellbeing of children. In doing so, we are also looking after our own wellbeing through exercising our professional autonomy.

As educators, we can reflect on the following questions:

- What prior experiences might have shaped this parent/child/staff member's sense of personal agency?
- How can I make it easier for them to communicate their views and to tell them how I have listened?
- How can I bring creativity into my work to support the wellbeing of the children and myself?

In much of our work, the focus is on the next achievement or goal. These reflective questions might help to highlight the progress you have already made towards increasing wellbeing in your setting.

Developing a Reflective Approach to Wellbeing and Involvement in Doncaster

Over the last few years in Doncaster, we have reviewed and changed much of the early years SEND documentation to place greater emphasis on wellbeing and involvement. We were fortunate as a service to access training on developing a Trauma Informed Approach in 2019, and since then we have set about reviewing processes, advice and strategies, prioritising wellbeing and promoting positive experiences for children over other areas of learning.

My colleague Mandy Haddock (Lead Early Years Inclusion Officer for SEND) initially integrated wellbeing scales into the Early Years Panel request referral documentation. This enabled a focus on requests for support being directly linked to children's wellbeing and engagement in learning. Key questions were:

- What difference will this support make to children's positive experiences?
- How will children's wellbeing and involvement be improved through the support requested?

This important shift in practice has led to many conversations with schools and settings about stripping back demands and refocusing on involvement and engagement, centring wellbeing at the heart of what we do.

Mandy and my colleague Sarah Thurston (Area SENCO) also devised a wellbeing plan to support early years providers to put belonging and self-regulation at the heart of planning provision.

Reflection over recent months has been key, and there has been a movement within our team in Doncaster to question previously well-intended strategies and consider whether they promote the wellbeing of the child. Many conversations with colleagues have examined whether previous strategies have promoted compliance to routine or activity completion over connection and wellbeing. Much consideration has been given towards the promotion of wellbeing over all other factors, and this has led to evolving practice.

Reflecting on Wellbeing and Involvement – A Case Study

A school I recently visited in central Doncaster sought help from our services due to an increase in the number of children who they had identified with possible SEND. The senior leaders in the school described the early years staff as being 'at breaking point'. They felt they had a unique cohort of children this year, who had very different needs to the cohorts that had previously attended the school. They described the children's behaviour as 'extremely difficult to manage'. This led to the staff feeling in crisis and unequipped to provide opportunities for children's learning and development.

My colleague Suzanne Walton (Lead Early Years Inclusion Officer for schools) and I met with the senior leaders in the school to establish what their priorities were and how we could support them to meet the needs of what they felt was their 'most challenging cohort'. It became apparent through these initial meetings that the school was delivering the routines and provision in the same way they had done year after year. Formal practice was so ingrained in the Reception classrooms that they felt there were barriers to developing change. Areas of provision had remained the same for many years and were a staple part of what they had delivered year in, year out. During a meeting with the early years team, we all quickly established that the provision was based around what the adults planned as their staple early years classroom rather than considering the individual learning profiles of the children accessing the environment.

We began by discussing their own wellbeing within the team. The saying 'You can't pour from an empty cup' seems to sum up how they were feeling. Everyone involved agreed that the team was feeling low. They had lost some of their enthusiasm due to their day jobs feeling like an uphill struggle and felt they needed to change practice to increase their own wellbeing and to feel more positive about their roles. We discussed ways we could support each other, leaning on one another to move practice forward.

My next step was a discussion to identify the most difficult times for the adults to manage children within the setting, and to analyse what was happening in those moments for the children and the adults. The practitioners quickly identified that the routine of the day was difficult for many of the children. Reflection led to a recognition that for much of the session practitioners were delivering whole-class adult-led lessons such as phonics, writing and maths, and they were observing children showing decreasing levels of concentration and engagement within these sessions.

The team also identified that their early years environment needed enhancement. They noticed that it offered limited opportunities for enquiry or exploration. Much of the environment was tabletop-focused and the format of the day was more typically primary-focused, with a routine which started with adult input at the beginning of the session, followed by tabletop 'work', followed by a short time to access continuous provision and then 'playtime' outside in the playground. Staff reported that they felt a number of children could not manage the routine and that it felt like the wrong 'fit' for them. Staff observed that some children would persistently become frustrated, which was demonstrated through their behaviours; examples included kicking out or casting aside resources.

The early years team felt that this lack of engagement prevented educators from delivering planned adult input, and instead they felt they were spending much of their time 'managing children's behaviour'. The staff identified that practice had to change but were unsure where to start. We discussed the importance of engagement through enjoyment and shared what staff had observed about individual children. We reflected on key questions: When did the children show high levels of wellbeing and involvement in their learning? When did they show joy in learning? I spoke to staff about the benefits of 'tuning in' to children and recommended that educators spend time, before my follow-up visit, observing children and noting when they demonstrated optimal levels of wellbeing and engagement.

Reflecting on Provision and Planning

On our following visit, we started by prioritising wellbeing and involvement and developing this as a strand that was reflected through each area of teaching and learning. Once we had established this as an approach and the staff team recognised the benefits, we began to support the setting by mapping areas of provision and a routine that allowed for increased opportunities to access provision, based on what practitioners had observed brought the children identified increased joy and high levels of involvement.

Key questions to consider were:

- How do you know the child is highly involved in an activity (acknowledging that this could look very different for neurodivergent children)?
- How can we extend and build on the involvement?
- How do we organise provision and routine to enable children to have more joyful experiences?

Conversations indicated that children show wellbeing in different ways, and it was crucial to have in-depth knowledge of a child's responses and profile to plan possible experiences.

By focusing initially on these aspects, the team identified that a number of the children showed higher levels of wellbeing and involvement in the outdoor area and in periods of child-led learning. The team also shared that, prior to my visit, they had not had the opportunity to focus closely on the learning profile of individual children, and they had focused mainly on fitting the group into their established routines and learning focus.

This took me back to a lightbulb moment I had experienced. I was fortunate 15 years ago to be part of an early years study group who visited Reggio Emilia in Italy. This experience had a profound impact on my career and approach to early education, and I often return to Loris Magaluzzi's well-known poem, 'The Hundred Languages of Children'. Many children follow a neurotypical pathway but many diverge. What truly resonates with me in Malaguzzi's poem is the message that *there is no one way to learn – there are a hundred ways.*

Suzanne and I began to work with the school on identifying areas for change. This involved developing the areas of continuous provision and extending the periods of time that identified children could access the outdoor environment and child-led learning. This refocused the provision on children's wellbeing and engagement.

Mapping the provision was challenging initially. The staff team had concerns: how would they enable identified children to access bespoke provision while still ensuring that typically developing children were also challenged and opportunities were provided to extend their learning?

Initially, we stripped the timetable back to basics and focused on the essential aspects of the routine. Snack time and playtime were removed from the timetable, and staff recognised that the previous routine was preventing children from developing their independence and accessing the outdoor area and child-led play for extended periods of time.

Educators were then deployed in different ways. Instead of supporting children to join in with adult-led phonics or maths input, they began to consider how to plan for individual next steps and outcomes by enabling neurodivergent children to access the outdoor area or continuous provision, with an educator scaffolding their learning, while an adult-led session took place elsewhere in the environment. They began to devise a plan of practitioners joining in and enhancing individual children's play, fostering their unique learning profile and personalised outcomes.

We visited the school a number of times following the provision mapping session, and they were excited to share with me the improvements that they had observed in increased wellbeing, engagement and involvement for those children whom they had previously found challenging and disengaged.

There were some huge successes. The team observed that children who had previously demonstrated little engagement were now excited to learn. The educators also showed increased levels of wellbeing. Seeing increased joy and engagement for children had reignited their passion for teaching in the early years. There is still lots that they want to change and develop, but they felt that prioritising wellbeing and involvement had been the right place to start.

In Doncaster, we have tried to develop more opportunities to support wellbeing for early years educators. In our own team meetings, which have taken some time to re-establish following the pandemic, we have tried to allocate time to talk about successes, celebrations, how we are feeling and how we can support each other, recognising the extreme pressures early education settings face.

When we deliver training, we seize opportunities to talk about wellbeing in the early years profession and ways we can increase this. We were fortunate to receive training from Kate Moxley (Wellness for All) in 2021, which has helped to put wellbeing firmly on the agenda.

Leaders and managers of Doncaster settings often share the ways they have been creative in their approach to keep morale high; examples have included wellbeing Wednesdays where practitioners are able to access a pamper treat, or boxes where educators are encouraged to write something positive about another member of staff to be shared with them. As expected, early years educators come up with some of the most creative ways to encourage joy in every day.

Thought Provocations

- Is child and adult wellbeing high on the agenda in your workplace?
- Are you aware of individual signs of wellbeing and involvement for your children?
- How do you support and maintain your own wellbeing?

References

Laevers, F. (2005) *Well-Being and Involvement in Care Settings. A Process-Oriented Self-Evaluation Instrument*. Kind & Gezin and Research Centre for Experiential Education Leuven University.

Moxley, K. (2023) A Beginner's Guide to Educator Wellbeing. https://tapestry.info/a-beginners-guide-to-educator-wellbeing-2.html

Child's Name

Wellbeing

Consider how you observe positive wellbeing for the individual child and their unique characteristics. Positive wellbeing could be recognised by a child feeling at ease, being spontaneous and free of emotional tensions. Considerations may be whether the child often looks happy and cheerful, smiles or cries out with pleasure. They may be lively and full of energy and spontaneous or expressive in their actions or show an openness to the environment. Playing with sounds, humming or singing may also be signs the child is relaxed not tense.

Notes

Actions

Copyright material from Ann Lowe and Stephen Kilgour (2025), *The Inclusive Early Years Educator*, Routledge

Child's Name

Involvement

High levels of involvement could be recognised by a child being intensely engaged, showing concentration, creativity, energy and persistence. They are not easily distracted and have intense moments in their exploration and play.

Reflect on whether they are truly engaged or just going 'through the motions' with a routine activity. A knowledge of the individual child is key – particularly for neurodivergent children.

Notes

Actions

Copyright material from Ann Lowe and Stephen Kilgour (2025), *The Inclusive Early Years Educator*, Routledge

Chapter 4

ANTI-RACIST PRACTICE

In order to help early years educators apply an anti-racist lens to their practice, we need to consider the ways that we deepen our understanding of what racism is, how it is baked into the society that we are a part of and how we can start to understand its impact systemically and interpersonally within the early years sector. Sharing, acknowledging and valuing the differences of children's lived experiences based on their racialised identities, cultures and ethnicities as significant parts of who they are is one aspect of this work. But we must also critically reflect on how our own intersecting identity markers have impacted how we have come to navigate society. If we do not see how we fit into the wider jigsaw puzzle of how this unequal society operates, then we will not be able to recognise when our own practice may be harmful – whether intentionally or unintentionally. It is important that we understand how racism is as much a safeguarding issue as other types of abuse and that we are equipped to identify these signifiers in the same way that we are trained to identify signs of physical, emotional and sexual abuse. The Covid-19 pandemic and the impact of the murder of George Floyd in the US by police officer Derek Chauvin led to the social uprisings of the Black Lives Matter protests, but they also led to much misunderstanding among those of us who had been oblivious to the hundreds of years of racism and social injustice that have plagued society globally.

Since 2004, Liz Pemberton had been managing an early years setting in Birmingham, England, which had been serving children and families who were predominantly Black. The geographical location of her nursery was partly the reason for this, but another significant factor was that her setting prided itself on having a deep understanding of the importance of cultural safety and competency when it came to engaging with the diversity of Black children and families that it attracted. Having had a long history of working in the sector, Liz's mother, Yvonne Kerr, had owned and managed children's day nurseries in Birmingham since 1987. But she had not done

DOI: 10.4324/9781003409618-5

so without challenging many forms of racism – from banks to local authorities, there were always racist hurdles and barriers.

Liz always ensured that Black children – who she recognised were experiencing the brunt of the impact of a racist society whether through education, healthcare or housing – were leaving her nursery with a positive sense of self. At the start of the pandemic in 2020, after 16 years of managing her nursery, Liz decided that she needed to pivot and spread the knowledge she had embedded within her early years setting about cultural safety and anti-racism. She has subsequently become a powerful voice in the early years sector, setting up her training and consultancy company, The Black Nursery Manager. Through her training courses, consultancy work and significant social media following, Liz challenges educators to rethink everything they thought they knew about how racism shows up in the sector, and how we must not conflate 'multiculturalism' or 'inclusion and diversity' with what anti-racist practice actually is. Liz defines anti-racist practice as making the conscious, consistent and intentional choice to challenge racism and disrupt the multitude of ways that it shows up in our practice and its presence within the systems and structures of the sector as a whole. Liz recognised that racism was often misunderstood within the sector as something that needn't be addressed because 'all early years educators were nice' and therefore couldn't be racist. Or the myth that children at such a young age did not start to see skin colour and attach a social value to that, yet it would be taken as a given that these same children were able to recognise the different colours of their personal belongings such as coats or shoes. She wanted to ensure there was a way that educators could begin to grapple with their own understanding of racism, and so she set educators on this journey by devising the 4 Es of anti-racist practice:

Embrace all children's racial, cultural and religious backgrounds.
Embed a culture of belonging and value among practitioners and children.
Ensure that practice is culturally sensitive and that the child is positioned as the expert of their own identity.
Extend learning opportunities for the child by showing interest, expanding conversations and using culturally appropriate resources.

Liz has written 'A Beginner's Guide to Anti-Racism' which is a free resource that can be downloaded by scanning Figure 4.1.

This chapter will explore the importance of anti-racist practice in the EYFS. It is important to reiterate that the two authors of this book are white, and so throughout

FIGURE 4.1 A QR code linking to 'A Beginner's Guide to Anti-Racism'

this chapter we have tried to focus on the messages and experiences of Black and Brown educators.

Understanding Racism

To be an anti-racist practitioner, you first need to understand the many different forms that racism can take and that it is deeply embedded in the history of our society.

(Lumsden, 2023, p.14)

Structural racism: laws, rules, or official policies in a society that result in and support a continued unfair advantage to some people and unfair or harmful treatment of others based on race. (Cambridge Dictionary, 2024a)

Structural racism refers to the systematic oppression of ethnic minorities that leads to the disparities that we see in terms of income, employment, health, etc. So the disproportionate death rates from Covid are an example of structural racism, caused by the place we [ethnic minorities] find ourselves in society.

(Andrews, 2021)

Institutional racism: policies, rules, practices, etc. that are a usual part of the way an organization works, and that result in and support a continued unfair advantage to some people and unfair or harmful treatment of others based on race. (Cambridge Dictionary 2024b)

Institutional racism refers to how racism is practised through the institutions such as schools, universities, workplaces in ways that maintain structural racism.

(Andrews, 2021)

Here is an example of institutional racism in the early years from Jane Lane who first describes a familiar scenario:

An early years setting that operates a waiting list and offers places on a first-come-first-served basis, with those at the top of the list having priority, may well be operating institutional racism.

(Lane, 2022)

This might initially seem a completely fair practice, but Jane explains why that might not be the case:

[F]amilies who are unfamiliar with the concept of waiting lists or the way early years services are organised, or do not yet live in the area, do not put their children's names down as early as others.

(Lane, 2022)

And so:

This means that their children will be lower on the list and so will be less likely to gain a place than children from families who are familiar with the system.

(Lane, 2022)

In her book *Young Children and Racial Justice* (2008), Jane Lane provides a more extensive list of the different types of racism and how they operate in the early years.

White Privilege

The vast majority of educators in the early years are white (DfE, 2023). It is therefore vital that those who work in the sector are aware of their own privileges before embarking on anti-racist practice in their settings or schools.

White privilege does not mean that you will have never faced any form of discrimination or prejudice, but it does mean that one of the reasons that you won't have faced discrimination or prejudice is because of the colour of your skin. In a society that has racism baked into it, the ways in which racism shows up may not always be obvious to you because if you are white, you may have just always thought of particular things as normal. For example, the entire team of staff at your child's nursery being all white yet the majority of the children who attend being of South Asian heritage.

(Pemberton, 2022, p.5)

There can be a backlash to the notion of white privilege, particularly when linked to socio-economic status, but it is important to reinforce that having white privilege does not mean that a person has not suffered from other disadvantages.

Talking About Race

In order for us to successfully talk about race, it is important that we first consider our own racial literacy. If we have a good level of racial literacy, we are much more likely to feel confident when exploring and discussing themes of race. There are no shortcuts to increasing our awareness and understanding; it is necessary to devote time to this vitally important area.

Anna Freud have a useful free guide around developing racial literacy for those working in education. It signposts a number of helpful books, videos and articles and can be accessed by scanning Figure 4.2.

Talking about race is a first step in countering racism. It is a mistaken assumption that treating all people in the same way and ignoring differences in race is a sufficient response to racism. This approach simply allows the continuation of bias in society which disadvantages people from Black and minoritised groups. Instead of a colour-blind approach to race, more proactive anti-racism is needed.

(Early Years Coalition, 2021)

Particularly for white educators, talking about race with young children may feel challenging. For a long time, taking a position that we were blind to the colour of a child's skin seemed to be the go-to approach for those of us working in nurseries or

FIGURE 4.2 A QR code linking to Anna Freud's racial literacy guide

schools. After all, if we took this stance, we could avoid difficult questions that we didn't necessarily know the 'right' answer to. Unfortunately, this strategy is not only misguided but potentially harmful to the children we teach. 'When adults are silent about race, children's racial prejudice and misconceptions can be maintained or reinforced' (Early Years Coalition, 2021).

The key way for educators to become more capable of facilitating and enabling important conversations about race is through high-quality training. Once we better understand the structural racism that is present in our education system, we begin to appreciate the importance of proactive anti-racist practice in our setting or school.

It might be that conversations naturally occur during play with our children, but it is important that we also provide opportunities for discussions to take place. It might be that we enable thought provocations in the resources that we provide – dolls with different colour skin, for example, should be commonplace. It could be that we encourage children to think about differences in the characters from the books on offer. Alternatively, we might intentionally embark on dialogue about skin colour through the use of a resource like *My Skin, Your Skin* by Laura Henry-Allain which approaches the subject head-on.

Conversations about race should not be reserved for nurseries or schools in ethnically diverse areas of the country. It is the responsibility of every setting to facilitate learning in this area, so that every child can understand their part in an equitable society. And so it is important that we all think about anti-racist training and appropriate resourcing in our provision.

The Importance of Representation

As previously mentioned, the resources in our setting or school need to have been given careful thought. Crucially, all educators working in our space need to understand why this is so important – and actively engage with the diverse range on offer.

Unfortunately, Black or Brown children have been much less likely to see themselves represented in picture books than their white peers. There may have been some token representation, but it was extremely rare for the hero or star of the book to be anything other than white. Imagine the messaging that this sends to young children who are from minoritised communities. Conversely, consider how powerful it must feel for them to see characters that they can relate to in books that are shared in school. Thankfully, there has been a significant increase in the representation of Black and Brown characters in children's books over recent years, with many specialist suppliers. There's never been a better time to source quality books that deliver 'they look like me' moments. Of course, representation isn't exclusive to race. We must ensure that we are also considering books that contain neurodivergent or disabled characters and same-gendered families – the representation of all children and all communities. Never stop thinking about the very big messages that your little library sends to children and families in your setting.

A further aspect of representation that can often be overlooked is the makeup of our staff teams. The chances of a Black or Brown child feeling a genuine sense of belonging in a nursery or school where every educator is white are likely to be decreased. It is also hugely beneficial for all children in a setting to see a diverse range of adults working there. It is vital that leaders in our education establishments seriously reflect on this if we are to be truly inclusive.

It is not always straightforward to ensure that a diverse range of applications are received when recruiting new staff, and this can obviously vary significantly depending on the part of the country in which you are based. Regardless of your location, the aspiration to employ a diverse team should be a high priority. The advantages are profound, particularly when we think about our children with learning differences. If we are to foster a sense of belonging for every child, then having educators in any stage of education who our children/students can relate to or find comfort with is potentially life-changing. The notion that someone who 'looks like me' can hold positions of authority – and all those working in our education settings do hold authority in the eyes of children and their families – in itself provides a wealth of inspiration.

If, as a leader or manager, you are struggling to attract diverse applicants for your vacancies, are there particular places where you haven't previously advertised which may encourage a wider range of applicants? If the process isn't successful in drawing a range of submissions, *don't give up* – try something different next time. Connect with local members of the communities that you hope will apply and make it clear that you aim to inspire every child in your care with outstanding members of staff who have a rich variety of lived experiences.

The Black SEND Index

Marguerite Haye and Emma Pinnock are two Black educators who are striving to improve representation across the SEND sector. They were all too aware of the lack of Black professionals working with children who have learning differences and disabilities, and the impact this has on families. Emma and Marguerite decided to create a resource which early years settings and schools could use to find Black professionals working in the sector.

> The child should be at the centre. We know what the data says. The outcomes for disabled Black children are very poor. The Black SEND Index will give us the chance to speak alongside parents to empower their voices.
>
> *(Haye, 2023)*

You can download the Black SEND Index by scanning Figure 4.3.

FIGURE 4.3 A QR code linking to the Black SEND Index

The MANDELA Model Workbook

The MANDELA Model was developed by Dr Prospera Tedam in 2011. It was developed following research that Prospera had undertaken into the experiences of Black African students studying social work in the UK. It was created to support more effective supervision and support of these students. Around this time, Prospera's colleague Professor Eunice Lumsden realised that this could also be a very effective tool for early childhood settings. After many years of discussions and ideas, Professor Lumsden released the MANDELA Model Workbook in 2023. The intention of the workbook is to support early years leaders in developing belonging for families and staff in their setting's community.

Each of the letters in MANDELA frames questions to help facilitate a deep analysis of practice and address sensitive issues that are integral to any work that focuses on a holistic approach to inclusivity from a place of compassion and care:

Make time
Acknowledge
Needs
Differences

Educational experiences

Life experiences

Age

Scan Figure 4.5 to download the MANDELA Model Workbook.

FIGURE 4.4 The cover of the MANDELA Model Workbook

FIGURE 4.5 A QR code linking to the MANDELA Model Workbook

Curriculum

The notion of curriculum in the early years has been a contentious issue in recent times. Some educators are of the view that learning in the formative years should be entirely child-led, whereas others feel that this should be balanced with periods of more direct teaching. What can't be disputed is the fact that as educators to the youngest children in our education system, we have the opportunity to guide their learning at a very important stage of their development. This will most likely be through the resources we provide and the interactions that we offer.

Regardless of your views on more or less formal approaches, we all have an idea of what we want our children to learn. In maths, for example, we know that ultimately we want our children to be able to count securely. In literacy, we hope that our children will be able to write their name and so we offer them the appropriate building blocks for them to achieve this. When it comes to their social development, we need to give our children the appropriate tools to celebrate and embrace difference – not just tolerate it. We can do this through resources and through conversations fuelled by high-quality staff training. But in order for this work to be meaningful, it needs to be embedded into every aspect of our teaching and learning. Each and every day, are we thinking about what and who our children see? What music do they hear? What foods do they taste?

It is important that we take time to reflect on our provision and particularly our learning environment to ensure that we strive for the sense of belonging that all of our children need if they are to thrive in nursery or school.

Educator's View – Rachna Joshi, Early Years Consultant

When discussing the importance of anti-racist practice for our youngest learners, we need to understand the impact of racism on individuals and as a collective within society. Racism is traumatic, and the prolonged exposure to racial trauma in our everyday lives impacts our physical, emotional and mental health. There has been further research into prolonged trauma having an impact on the levels of cortisol in the body and how this in turn impacts brain development and physical health. Ultimately, anti-racist practice can save lives.

Representation is crucial for young children. When we start with what the learner knows, we begin to understand what children are influenced by and exposed to in the world. By having wide representation, we provide children with ideas of what they can be – 'you can only be what you can see'. So as part of anti-racist practice, ensuring that children are seeing positive representations of people who look, behave, think and act like them has an impact on racial identity which is so vital for developing self-esteem, a positive sense of pride and academic achievement as researched by the Anna Freud Centre.

Many areas across the UK have little diversity within settings and schools, and the children in these areas may not have come across any groups racialised as Black or Brown before. Therefore, it is even more important that these children take on an anti-racist outlook as they need to understand that often they absorb and partake in a white supremacist society.

Although it might seem that anti-racism only looks at those racialised as Black and Brown, it is in fact inclusive of all marginalised groups, as progress for all can only be achieved when there is no further oppression on any group (Friere). Therefore, we need to consider the intersectionalities within anti-racist practice, race, gender, class and sexuality – for example, thinking about the range of challenges that working-class, same-gendered families may face.

When developing anti-racist practice in our schools and settings, we have to make sure that all staff are well trained in this area. The role of the adult is vital in ensuring children are represented, understood and responded to appropriately. Educators must consider how challenging situations need to be sensitively handled, as well as ensuring positive relationships with children are developed to support empathising with children, their families and understanding their contexts.

Children have the capacity for empathy and deep understanding of challenging concepts. Racism is learned, and therefore it can be unlearned, but this requires self-awareness, critical reflection and constant questioning. It is probably a lifelong process of unlearning due to the complexities of racism within society.

Educator's View continued – Rachna Joshi, Early Years Consultant

Observation and reflection

A little girl (T) of South Asian heritage was in my setting. It was a hot day and the children had taken off their jumpers. Another child came up to T and said, 'Your arms are hairy!' T looked at her arms and tried to hide them. The practitioners (R and D) noticed this interaction and tried to console her, showing that their arms were hairy too.

Later on, the practitioners reflected on this interaction. R discussed that there was a lot to unpick in that situation. Hairy bodies in South Asian communities are seen as undesirable, and these feelings and views have colonial roots. R herself shared that since she was a child, she had plucked, tweezed, waxed and lasered her body hair, and in that interaction, she had to reflect on her own views of body hair to ensure that T was left feeling beautiful. This might not have been enough to stop the damage of these outward consistent messages from society, but hopefully it was enough to help T in that moment.

In this observation, you can see the impact of external views on children's self-esteem; these consistent messages need to be reflected on and then responded to. In addition to the practitioner's interactions with T, they could also include photos of body and facial hair on women within the setting to provoke questions and ensure children see that body hair is natural and normal and nothing to be ashamed of.

Developing a Reflective Approach to Equity and Diversity in Doncaster

The murder of George Floyd, an African-American man who was murdered by a white police officer on 25 May 2020 in Minneapolis reverberated around the world. Floyd's death was a horrific example of systemic racism, which refers to the way race disadvantages people of colour in the criminal justice system. The murder and subsequent actions of the police galvanised people worldwide to protest against racism and discrimination and prompted much discussion on racial justice.

In Doncaster at this time, we were beginning to live with the government Covid restrictions, and many of the Doncaster Local Authority teams, whose usual day job was to visit, support and advise schools and settings, were now working for the majority of time from their homes. This fostered an opportunity of reflection across the sector and a range of working groups were set up to consider and improve current practice across education to prompt change. I was interested in joining the Equity and Diversity working group representing early years to learn more about how I could improve my practice and understanding, aiming to champion an improved approach.

Sameena Choudry (Learning Standards and Effectiveness Officer, Learning and Opportunities at Doncaster Council) led the group, which was made up of a number of representatives from different teams across the local authority as well as senior leaders in schools and settings across Doncaster. When we initially met, Sameena was in the process of finishing her first book, *Equitable Education: What everyone working in education should know about closing the attainment gap for all pupils.*

In the short time I had been working in Doncaster, I had met Sameena through a range of collaborative meetings, but the Equity and Diversity group was my first opportunity to get to know her better. In the initial meeting, I was immediately struck by Sameena's passion and dedication to improving equity for all. Sameena was a powerhouse of knowledge and spoke inspirationally about change. I went away from that first meeting with a deepening knowledge and understanding of injustice. Feeling grateful and excited to be part of the group and with a renewed enthusiasm to do more, I began collaborating with colleagues in the early years team and beyond to further my understanding.

In November, Sameena secured Bennie Kara, author of *A Little Guide for Teachers: Diversity in Schools*, to deliver a session with Doncaster colleagues. Bennie's narratives and teaching continued to improve my understanding and at the same time prompted me to seek more opportunities to learn.

One of the most powerful messages from these discussions was the disruption of the concept that by 'treating everyone the same' we can achieve equality for all.

In our first meeting, Sameena shared a popular visual image of Equity vs Equality. This was a moment of clarity in helping the group understand why treating everyone equally doesn't bring equity; equity can only be achieved through treating people differently.

> Knowing the difference between those terms is a brilliant starting point for teachers who wish to model diversity in the classroom. It is with this in mind that the individual teacher has to know the difference between equality and equity. The former teaches that everyone is the same. The latter acknowledges different starting points and asks society to create better stepping stones to successful futures.
>
> *(Kara, 2020)*

Stephen and I began discussing the importance of anti-racist practice as part of the Reflection Toolkit, and through our collaborative work I was able to learn much about early years professionals out there 'doing the work' to drive forward anti-racist practice. Stephen acknowledges the work of Liz Pemberton, the Black Nursery Manager earlier in this chapter. After my conversations with Stephen, I began to follow Liz's Instagram account. From this simple act of connection on social media, Liz's work really influenced my thinking about how to get the message out to the early years sector in Doncaster.

Liz talks about the need to get to a place of discomfort in order for practitioners to be able to be comfortable with having necessary conversations about race with adults and children in the early years. I began to set about reviewing and further developing a training package in Doncaster on Equity and Diversity in the early years which focused more specifically on anti-racist practice. *The tiney guide to becoming an inclusive, anti-racist educator*, co-written by Laura Henry-Allain MBE, published in 2021, also gave much food for thought.

I began delivering the training package in the 2021/2022 autumn term and have since worked closely with a number of early years settings and schools to develop this aspect of their practice. Much of the impact of this training is about really engaging with learning in this field of work and having necessary conversations about concepts such as privilege, discrimination and understanding the impact of systemic racism.

I recently spoke to Fledglings Nursery, who have a setting in both the east and south of Doncaster, and we discussed the impact of the training on their practice. Anna Dougherty, the owner and manager, shared with me the aspects they had changed in terms of ethos. Anna described how the team had really started to think about the message of belonging for families. They sought moments of connection to ask more questions about the families who come to the setting, and looked for opportunities to embrace aspects of their lives – inviting families in, learning about their customs and reflecting on the nursery environment to make sure it is representative of many ethnicities and cultures, striving towards every child and family feeling that they belong.

Embedding a Culture of Equity and Diversity – A Case Study

Around 18 months ago, I started on a journey to embed anti-racist practice across my two settings and improve our approach to equity and diversity. Historically, we had had some things in place, such as using children's home languages in our welcome songs and inviting parents in to share stories and songs; however, I knew that there was so much more that we could do. Both settings are in areas that are predominantly working-class and White British. We have a small number of children in each setting who speak English as an additional language.

The first step was to improve my own knowledge and understanding. To do this I attended an Equity and Diversity training session run by the local authority (Doncaster). I also began following Liz Pemberton (The Black Nursery Manager) on social media along with other useful accounts. The training and my related reading really galvanised me to want to do better to embrace all children's backgrounds and embed a culture of belonging for all our children.

Following the training, I carried out an equity and diversity audit of our environment, interactions and resources. This prompted me to answer questions such as 'Do we look at the range of skin colours in our setting and find the words to describe them in positive ways?' and 'Do black dolls portray a Black person accurately?' As a result, I ordered a range of new resources such as functional diversity small world figures.

I planned a staff training day to share what I had been learning with all my colleagues from both settings. We explored topics such as culture, prejudice, bias and vocabulary. We looked at the key texts that we use as part of our curriculum and made changes to include books more representative of a range of cultures, abilities and backgrounds. For example, we chose to include *Love Makes a Family* by Sophie Beer for our 2–3-year-olds and *My Shadow Is Pink* by Scott Stuart for our 3–5-year-olds.

Each room were given time to reflect on their environment and practice and create their own action plan which included items such as 'to increase the range of cooking equipment from all cultures'.

I also looked at ways in which we could learn more about our children and families, further supporting us to create a sense of belonging in our settings. I made some changes to our settle-in procedure, and instead of asking parents/carers to complete an 'All About Me' form when their child starts with us, we now invite them in for a 'settle-in conversation' with their child's key person. This allows the key person to sensitively ask questions about the child's family and experiences.

We built on this by asking parents and carers to donate food packaging and clothing from their homes for us to use in our role-play areas. When parents and carers speak another language in the home, we ask them to record key words/ phrases and short songs on recordable doors that we purchased from TTS. Children can then press the sound buttons to listen during continuous provision. We also asked parents to contribute ideas for our menu, allowing us to adapt our menu to better reflect the dietary habits of our families.

Each term, we plan the events that we will be celebrating (e.g., Eid, Pride), ensuring that this reflects the backgrounds of our children. We invite parents and carers to be involved – for example, by coming in to take part in an activity alongside the children.

Eighteen months on, I can see the impact of our journey so far. Staff report that they feel more secure in their use of vocabulary and ability to explore conversations that they may have previously avoided – for example, a child pointing out a difference in another child. Our peer observations reflect this, and we have examples of practitioners challenging stereotypes, such as 'Mummies don't play football'.

There's still plenty of work to do, and I feel we can go a lot further to improve our practice. I have recently appointed an 'equity and diversity' champion for each setting. My hope is that, with additional training, they will provide a point of contact for staff queries and questions as well as supporting staff with their inclusive practice.

Anna Dougherty (Fledglings Day Nursery)

Anna and her colleagues at Fledglings have been instrumental in spreading the message about anti-racist practice further in Doncaster, by sharing their journey at other early years training events. This has really given a sense of how Anna has embedded anti-racist practice as a whole-setting approach.

Reflecting on the 4 Es of Anti-Racist Practice in Doncaster

I refer to Liz Pemberton's 4 Es of anti-racist practice when delivering the Equity and Diversity training to early year educators; they are outlined in the section above. We advocate these four aspects in Doncaster as being a central part of the journey in embedding anti-racist practice. I worked with a school recently which, after attending the training, had started with the 4 Es of anti-racist practice as a way of auditing and reflecting on what was working well in their setting around equity and inclusion and what they could do better. The school had identified:

Embrace

What they do well?

- They use photographs of the families who attend the nursery as part of the welcome board, and within the domestic play area at child's height.

What could be better?

- Allocate time to talk to families about their individual customs and traditions when they start at the school. To embed this into practice by creating a culture of curiosity to find out more about each family, particularly if the child's heritage is in the minority in the setting.

Embed

What they do well?

- Books and songs reflect a range of cultures. Families who access the setting take part in telling/recording stories which are played to all children as part of everyday practice.

What could be better?

- Begin to gather a sense of team member's understanding of privilege. Have increased conversations about implicit bias and an understanding of how this affects judgement. Address this understanding and embed an approach of reflecting on issues with each other.

Ensure

What is working well?

- Staff expose children to a range of cultures and diverse celebrations, through planned opportunities to share resources, texts and music.

What could be better?

- Finding out more about the individual customs of each family. Don't make assumptions – *e.g. we have had a child from Nigeria before so they will have had the same lived experiences as other children from Africa and will be supported by the same resources.* Acknowledge cultural experience is authentic to each individual child and family and commit to learning more.

Extend

What is working well?

- Wide range of resources offered to children and within the environment and provision reflects a range of diverse ethnicities.

What could be better?

- Practitioners increasing opportunities to talk about the resources on offer and to lead children to recognise difference of skin colours, hair textures, etc. within these resources. Staff feeling confident to know why it is important to talk about difference. Use texts such as *My Skin, Your Skin* by Laura Henry-Allain as a starting point.

The school found the 4 Es a useful tool to start to think about what was already working well in their practice and what they needed to improve. What emerged was that although they felt they embraced multi-culturalism, this was mainly on the surface, and they had much to do to improve their approach to encourage curiosity, position themselves as learners, understand their own privilege and know that having the resources is not enough to develop children's understanding of equity – they need to have conversations with children.

Reflecting on the Journey of Developing Anti-Racism Practice

Many settings in Doncaster have started to reflect on their practice through an anti-racist lens, due to raising the importance of this reflection on practice. It is also true that there have been educators who have questioned the messages I have shared particularly around the understanding of privilege, inherent racism and the importance of treating people differently.

As identified in *The tiney guide to becoming an inclusive, anti-racist educator* by Laura Henry-Allain MBE and Matt Lloyd-Rose, being 'colour blind' is a common pitfall. 'We treat everyone the same regardless of difference' and 'We don't see colour, we welcome everyone here' are common threads to explore. Some educators have challenged the messages I have shared about introducing concepts such as 'prejudice', 'racism' and 'privilege' with young children and are uncomfortable with the notion of exposing children to knowledge of these concepts so young. The fact is discrimination exists in many forms, and having informed discussions about these concepts with the help of books and resources will pave the way for increased understanding of the ways to challenge prejudice in our society.

Opening up conversations about stereotype, bias and being fearful of the term 'racism' are then the place to restart, revisiting the message of 'feeling discomfort to get to a place of being comfortable to talk about race'. The experience in Doncaster is that we are all coming from different starting points on the journey, but the important part is being on the journey to reflect and learn more.

Thought Provocations

- Do you feel comfortable talking about race in your setting or school?
- Are you aware of your own privileges?
- How are you advocating for all children?

This chapter has been written with the support of Liz Pemberton, whose help we appreciate hugely.

References

Andrews, K. (2021) Racism is the public health crisis. *The Lancet 397*(10282), 1342–1343. https://doi .org/10.1016/S0140-6736(21)00775-3

Cambridge Dictionary (2024a) Structural racism. https://dictionary.cambridge.org/dictionary/english /structural-racism

Cambridge Dictionary (2024a) Institutional racism. https://dictionary.cambridge.org/dictionary/ english/institutional-racism

Department for Education (DfE) (2023) Childcare and early years provider survey. https://explore -education-statistics.service.gov.uk/find-statistics/childcare-and-early-years-provider-survey /2022

Haye, M. (2023) The Black SEND Index. The Foundation Stage Forum Podcast. https://fsf-podcasts .simplecast.com/episodes/the-black-send-index

Henry-Allain, L. and Lloyd-Rose, M. (2021) *The tiney guide to becoming an inclusive, anti-racist educator.* https://start.tiney.co/tiney-inclusion-guide

Kara, B. (2020) *A Little Guide for Teachers: Diversity in Schools*. SAGE Publications.

Lane, J. (2008) *Young Children and Racial Justice: Taking Action for Racial Equality in the Early Years – Understanding the Past, Thinking about the Present, Planning for the Future*. London: National Children's Bureau.

Lane, J. (2022) Institutional Discrimination in the Early Years. *The Therapeutic Care Journal*, 1 October. https://thetcj.org/in-residence-articles/institutional-discrimination-in-the-early-years-by-jane -lane

Lumsden, E. (2023) A Curriculum that Promotes Equality and Challenges Racism and Sexism. In J. Grenier and C. Vollans (eds) *Putting the EYFS Curriculum into Practice*. SAGE. https://uk.sagepub .com/en-gb/eur/putting-the-eyfs-curriculum-into-practice/book281603

Pemberton, L. (2022) A Beginner's Guide to Anti-Racism. Tapestry. https://tapestry.info/a-beginners -guide-to-anti-racism.html

The Early Years Coalition (2021) *Birth to 5 Matters: Non-Statutory Guidance for the Early Years Foundation Stage*. https://birthto5matters.org.uk/wp-content/uploads/2021/03/Birthto5Matters -download.pdf

Child's Name

Anti-Racist Practice

In order to promote and value diversity, we need to consider ways of sharing and celebrating children's lived experiences. It is important that we are considerate of each child's varied circumstances.

Representation

Can children see themselves and their families represented in the environment? How is this happening?

Actions

Copyright material from Ann Lowe and Stephen Kilgour (2025), *The Inclusive Early Years Educator*, Routledge

Child's Name

Anti-Racist Practice

In order to promote and value diversity, we need to consider ways of sharing and celebrating children's lived experiences. It is important that we are considerate of each child's varied circumstances.

Educator Learning

How are you ensuring that you are learning about structural and institutional racism? What are you doing in your setting or school to ensure that important conversations about racism are taking place?

Actions

Copyright material from Ann Lowe and Stephen Kilgour (2025), *The Inclusive Early Years Educator*, Routledge

Chapter 5

CHARACTERISTICS OF EFFECTIVE TEACHING AND LEARNING

The 2012 iteration of Development Matters, produced by Early Education as non-statutory guidance for the Early Years Foundation Stage, was the reason that the phrase 'characteristics of effective learning' (or CoEL) became commonplace in nurseries and schools across the country.

Characteristics of Effective Learning
Playing and exploring – engagement Finding out and exploring Playing with what they know Being willing to 'have a go'
Active learning – motivation Being involved and concentrating Keeping trying Enjoying achieving what they set out to do
Creating and thinking critically – thinking Having their own ideas Making links Choosing ways to do things

(Moylett & Stewart, 2012, p.5)

The intention of the characteristics was to help us think more deeply about *how* children learn, rather than just *what* they learn. One of the authors of the guidance, Nancy Stewart, influenced their inclusion and wrote extensively on the theme in her 2011 book, *How Children Learn: The Characteristics of Effective Early Learning*.

The characteristics of effective learning represent the active role children adopt as they follow their curiosity and push themselves to become more competent and understand more, and are rewarded by the inner satisfaction of mastering new skills and feeling their independence grow. These learning dispositions, behaviours and habits of mind are particularly important in the EYFS because they build the

DOI: 10.4324/9781003409618-6

foundations needed to support children to become strong lifelong learners and independent thinkers (Early Years Coalition, 2021).

When the 2020 version of Development Matters was released by the Department for Education, the word 'teaching' was added to the phrase.

The Importance of Self-Regulation and Co-Regulation

The 'Birth to 5 Matters' guidance states that 'Children's emotional wellbeing is the first necessity for effective learning' (Early Years Coalition, 2021). So, if emotional regulation is at the forefront of your thinking, and you also observe the characteristics of effective learning taking place, then the likelihood is that you are providing a high-quality environment for learning.

We discussed the importance of wellbeing in Chapter 3, but it is vital that as educators we understand self-regulation and co-regulation, and how they work together. A reminder of our definitions from earlier in the book:

> Self-regulation refers to our ability to manage our responses and reactions to feelings and things that may be happening to us.

> Co-regulation refers to the way parents or key people in a child's life support them to self-regulate. This may be through calming words or actions and generally being 'present' in the moment of stress. This co-regulation helps a child become more adept at their own self-regulation skills over time.

One of the biggest mistakes we can make in the early years is to strive for self-regulation in our children before they are ready. Older children and many adults still struggle with regulating their own emotions when they are distressed. As with any teaching and learning, we should meet a child where they are. To leave a young person in a state of distress in order for them to 'deal with it themselves' is not OK. The fact that moments of distress can often lead to heightened emotions for everyone present also gives us an opportunity to model how we regulate ourselves as well as support the children around us.

Co-regulation can be even more important for children with learning differences. We must reflect on and make changes to the language we use around challenging circumstances. To label moments of distress as 'meltdowns', 'tantrums' or just plain old 'bad behaviour' does a huge disservice to the emotions that the child in question is experiencing. Reframing what is being experienced can have a huge impact on the way that we respond to a situation. As educators, we need to be empathetic and use our knowledge of each child to support them as sensitively as we can, whether that is while playing together in the sand, learning to put a coat on or coping with emotions that overwhelm.

Educator's View – Ben Case (Education Advisor and experienced Reception teacher)

I always found that learning was truly embedded if the child was fully engaged. There is plenty of evidence to back up that children learn best through play, and so by allowing play to happen in the provision, we achieve the best outcomes.

One popular activity in my provision was leaving a box of magnets on a table, with a few different materials. The plan was that the children could use the magnets to explore which materials they 'stuck' to, but what I found was that the children started thinking about what they were seeing and actively searching for things in the provision that the magnets were 'sticking' to. The excitement when a child discovered something new that was 'sticky' spread through the class quickly. As adults, we could then introduce appropriate vocabulary such as 'attract' and also model sorting materials into those that the magnets were attracted to and those that weren't. We provided coloured labels for the children to attach to objects, and the environment became a sea of colour as they labelled things and shared their discoveries.

This was only possible because the children were given the freedom to be creative and to explore the resources without being told what to do or what couldn't be done with them. My confidence in allowing this to happen came from my own understanding that not everyone approaches an activity in the same way, and that the outcome may not always be what I expected. For me, the learning that took place was more important than the end product. If a child developed a valuable skill during the process, then I was happy. It may not produce a uniform display, but each child in my class was different, so I wouldn't expect or seek uniformity anyway. Planning a provision that meets their developmental progress, ensuring that I am aware of any child who may need extra support to access the provision, meant that every child was given the best chance to develop from their own starting point.

Playing and Exploring

All of us who work with young children know that everyone learns in unique ways. We also know that playing and exploring is the most effective means to learning (whisper it – not just for under-5s!). Not only do we learn differently, but we also explore environments and play differently. It is our role as educators in the early years to provide environments that are engaging for all. When we work with children with learning differences, we sometimes over-complicate things when it comes to our provision. Just as we would for any other child, we should observe what interests and motivates a child and adjust our environment accordingly to make it even more fascinating for them – all with the goal of encouraging learning. The distinction is that we usually need to spend more time observing a child with learning differences and invest more energy in 'tuning in' to their individuality.

As we have already covered, the key to a fulfilling and successful learning experience is *engagement*. Regardless of our age or stage in life, when we are engaged in something, we are more likely to make progress.

In 2011, Barry Carpenter developed a tool entitled the 'Engagement Profile and Scale'. It was designed to be used in specialist provision and the EYFS as a way of focusing on a child's engagement and prompting child-centred reflection on how to increase the learner's engagement, and therefore deepen learning.

> Sustainable learning can occur only when there is meaningful engagement. The process of engagement is a journey which connects a child and their environment (including people, ideas, materials and concepts) to enable learning and achievement.
>
> *(Carpenter, 2011, p. 2)*

The Engagement Profile and Scale is a helpful addition to your observational toolkit and provides opportunities to consider seven different 'engagement indicators':

- Awareness
- Curiosity
- Investigation
- Discovery
- Anticipation
- Initiation
- Persistence

You can find the tool and accompanying guidance by scanning Figure 5.1.

FIGURE 5.1 A QR code linking to the Engagement Profile and Scale

Video is increasingly used in the EYFS to record and share moments of progress and learning with families, but it can also be a powerful tool for self-reflection and analysis for educators. Reviewing footage of a child at play can lead to insightful discussions among staff teams, and using prompts like the Engagement Profile and Scale can lead to purposeful and substantial adaptations in our provision.

When considering our environment, we should also have an awareness of the unique and diverse range of identities of our children. How can we be inclusive in our provision, to ensure that all of our children have the confidence to be themselves while at their setting or school?

Children, just like adults, are capable of complex 'code-switching', continuously adapting their language, attitude and behaviour to various social settings and relationships. However, this becomes much more difficult when one important reference group (e.g. at the kindergarten) overtly or covertly, consciously or unconsciously conveys messages that another important reference group (e.g. in the home), is not accepted. Young children can all too often feel confronted with a forced choice, that identity is a matter of 'either/or' instead of a more inclusive 'and/and' that respects their multiple identities (Vandenbroeck in Brooker and Woodhead, 2008, p.26).

In her 'Beginner's Guide to Intersectionality in the Early Years' (2023), Warda Farah gives advice as to how we can be more inclusive in our environment:

> Young children who come from marginalised backgrounds can benefit greatly from a safe space that is free of judgement and prejudice. To achieve this, educators must be empathetic to the needs and experiences of their students, and actively work towards creating an inclusive learning environment. This can involve implementing inclusive curriculum and language, promoting diversity and celebrating differences, and providing resources and support for students who

FIGURE 5.2 A QR code linking to the Beginner's Guide to Intersectionality in the Early Years

may need it. By taking these steps, educators can help ensure that all students feel valued, seen, and heard.

Warda's guide is free to download and can be found by scanning Figure 5.2.

Active Learning

The central behaviour linked to this learning characteristic is *motivation*. Once a child has shown engagement, how can we maintain their **involvement**? There is an obvious link here to the Leuven Scale that we covered in Chapter 3.

When considering a child's level of involvement or **concentration**, we need to be open to the fact that the signs of this motivation won't necessarily look the same for all children. It is important to note that an autistic child, for example, might show signs of concentration or motivation in fewer areas of play than their neurotypical peers. However, their ability to focus and maintain concentration in these areas may well be greater.

It can be easy when planning our provision to fall into the trap of focusing on the wrong aspect of the special interest of a child. Perhaps a child loves playing with cars – we may think, 'If I make everything cars themed, then they are likely to be interested.' It can be more useful, however, to consider what the child is actually doing in their play with the cars.

Other key behaviours that are often associated with this particular characteristic are **persistence** and **satisfaction**. When we notice a child being persistent, we usually see them adapting their ideas or approaches and showing some resilience if things are not working as expected. Co-regulation skills will support learners to persevere and find ways to respond to disappointment. These skills could well be particularly important if working with a child who has learning differences.

Satisfaction is an area where, again, we need to consider each of our children as unique. Are we aware what the signs of satisfaction might look like for different children? Think about satisfaction as the fulfilment of a child's needs or expectations. As with any aspect of early education, getting to know our children as well as possible will give us the best chance of noticing this response.

Creating and Thinking Critically

The three subheadings for the final characteristic of effective teaching and learning are:

- Having their own ideas
- Making links
- Choosing ways to do things.

There is a common thread of **problem-solving** running throughout this characteristic. Our children with learning differences may well have alternative solutions, and these should not be dismissed.

This area in particular requires us, as inclusive educators, to broaden our horizons as to what play 'should' or 'needs to' look like. We must be cautious of the notion of 'high-quality play' as defined by neurotypical adults. For example, do we judge traditional practices such as role-play as the gold standard at our settings? It is vital that we consider our definitions carefully.

This idea of expanding our play borders could potentially allow us to think more broadly about the types and features of play, and this could lead to more inclusive approaches for SEND. Whether or not to define play remains tricky, but what I believe we can do is begin to reimagine play and develop more curiosity about the diverse ways of playing. This could potentially lead us to a more play-rich pedagogy which welcomes all its players (Murphy, 2022, p.183).

The essence of creativity is surely being open to thinking about and interpreting things in ways we hadn't considered previously. We need to make sure that we are open to learning ourselves, and to the possibilities of play when limitations and judgements aren't placed upon it.

It is worth repeating that until we tune in to the children in our setting or school and try to understand more about the play decisions they make, we are unlikely to be able to support them effectively in their learning.

Developing a Reflective Approach to the Characteristics of Effective Teaching and Learning in Doncaster

Visiting different children and settings every day is one of the reasons I love my role as Early Years Inclusion Officer in Doncaster. I'm passionate about finding out more about the unique nature of each child, building curiosity about how they learn and how we can increase their access to learning. I am in the privileged position to be able to devote time to observe children intensely, find out about what and how a child shows joy in learning and observe many of the ways they make the characteristics of effective learning a living, breathing concept. I feel very lucky to be able to share that joy in learning with you over the next few pages!

A little context...

The children I visit in settings and schools have usually been referred to our service by the provider because they have identified that the child has some barriers to learning and they would like some support with how to improve the child's access to learning through more specialist advice and collaborative thought.

The process of referral to our service involves the SENCO in the setting or school completing information about a child and their learning profile and submitting it to the monthly Early Years Panel, who determine what support would be most appropriate for the setting and the child.

The child I am describing in the next few pages has therefore been identified as having a special educational need or disability. I make reference to this point to identify the problem with the term SEND in general. Before we even set eyes on any of these children, they have already been identified as having 'needs', deficits that require fixing. In Doncaster over the last few years, we have been working hard to change our approach, to flip the narrative of deficit and to centre strengths-based language and vocabulary when describing children referred to the Early Years Panel. It has been an intense, sometimes challenging couple of years, but the tide is turning. Many Doncaster schools and settings have wholeheartedly embraced a neurodiversity-affirming approach.

I delivered training on the Reflection Toolkit at a staff meeting in one such setting in the spring term. I was surprised and delighted when I received this email in the morning:

Good Morning,

Where do I start...what a night of training.

I really wanted the staff to understand that this is a completely new way of thinking for us and inspire them to want to change their practice. You did this and so much more...

The feedback from the girls has been amazing.

It has totally changed the way we think and in time we hope to really look at our approach when working with neurodivergent children.

You really have put the spark back into a time where days are long and hard and keeping staff motivated is challenging.

Here are just a few of the comments staff sent me last night:

'That training last night was amazing'

'I loved it, really made me think of AM and how we need to be there to support when he goes to school'

'It made me go from wanting out completely, to wanting to go further, thank you'

The buzz in the nursery this morning is high and that's thanks to you.

Really grateful for you taking the time.

Thank you
Stacey Wilburn, Manager, Sunny Bright Day Nursery

I feel this says it all. I'm so grateful to every educator in Doncaster who has listened to me banging on my neurodiversity-affirming drum, and I couldn't be prouder of them for embarking on the journey of change to view children with SEND with a celebratory approach. It feels like an exciting time in Doncaster!

Reflecting on Playing and Exploring – A Case Study

- Finding out and exploring
- Using what they know in their play
- Being willing to have a go

Suki had been at her current setting for 12 months when she was referred by the setting to the Early Years Panel. Suki's attendance at the setting was less than 50 per cent, so the setting's first aim was to increase attendance. Although still only at 70 per cent when I visited, there had been a consistent pattern of attendance, and the staff team were able to build a picture of Suki's learning profile. They had referred Suki to the Early Years Panel to gain some additional funding for a practitioner to work in enhanced ratios for some of the time Suki was in nursery, to try to develop her communication and increase her access to the learning opportunities on offer in the setting.

On the day I visited Suki, she used physical prompts to communicate that she wanted to access the outdoor area, by moving a practitioner's hand to the door handle a few times. Over the course of the morning, it was clear that Suki had a preference for accessing the outdoor area. She particularly enjoyed running from one end to the other, and feeling the trees and bushes. Suki babbled with joy when she pulled her hands through the leaves.

After a few minutes of observation, I noticed that Suki had a pattern to her movements outdoors. She would run round the perimeter of the outdoor area, knock over a bin when she reached the near side and then run her fingers through the trees and bushes when she reached the far side. Suki used melodic babble which sounded 'songlike'.

I began to follow Suki, attempting to feel the same experience that she did, positioning myself as a learner about what Suki found joy in. I observed that Suki seemed to find delight in knocking the bin over. Suki would reach out and push the bin each time she reached it and she babbled delightedly as it fell over. The practitioners stood the bin up each time and said, 'Stop, Suki' and Suki delighted in knocking it over again and again. I replaced the bin with a stack of outdoor bricks, moving the resources to where the bin was originally placed. I modelled knocking over the bricks while moving around the environment with Suki.

Suki began to knock over the bricks each time, expressing delight in seeing them fall down. I began singing a building song (a made-up one…'Build it high!') and encouraged other children to build the tower. Suki continued to knock the tower down a couple of times, but on the third run round, she stopped and began building with the bricks to make a tower and then knocked the tower down. Suki started to build alongside the other children, smiling and babbling as she built up the bricks and knocked them over. I sang the building song, and Suki's babble became louder and more melodic. When I built anticipation by saying, 'Ready to knock it down?' Suki waited, looked at me and then knocked the bricks over.

The practitioners reported that this was the first time they had ever seen Suki play with bricks. Suki had never accessed the resource before. By the end of the session,

Suki had become so engaged in the bricks that she was beginning to take turns with other children and showed motivation to continue using the resource. Towards the end of the outdoor session, I supported Suki and a group of children to put the bricks back in the area they had come from. Suki transported the bricks back to the area and began accessing the other enhancements in this area.

During my visit, I spoke to Suki's key person and the SENCO at the setting about Suki's different learning profile. I agreed to lead a staff meeting with the SENCO about the Reflection Toolkit and understanding and celebrating neurodivergent play.

FIGURE 5.3 An example page from Suki's Reflection Toolkit.

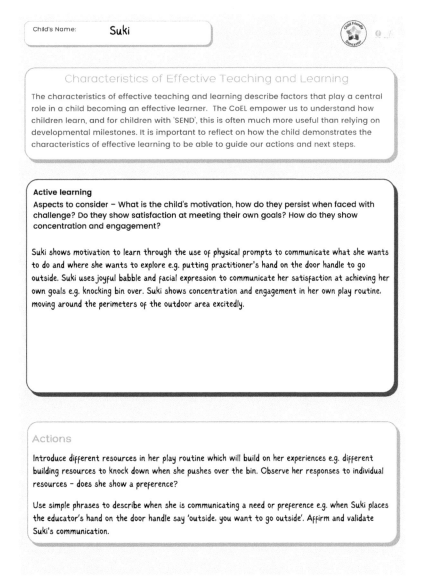

Child's Name: **Suki**

Characteristics of Effective Teaching and Learning

The characteristics of effective teaching and learning describe factors that play a central role in a child becoming an effective learner. The CoEL empower us to understand how children learn, and for children with 'SEND', this is often much more useful than relying on developmental milestones. It is important to reflect on how the child demonstrates the characteristics of effective learning to be able to guide our actions and next steps.

Active learning

Aspects to consider – What is the child's motivation, how do they persist when faced with challenge? Do they show satisfaction at meeting their own goals? How do they show concentration and engagement?

Suki shows motivation to learn through the use of physical prompts to communicate what she wants to do and where she wants to explore e.g. putting practitioner's hand on the door handle to go outside. Suki uses joyful babble and facial expression to communicate her satisfaction at achieving her own goals e.g. knocking bin over. Suki shows concentration and engagement in her own play routine, moving around the perimeters of the outdoor area excitedly.

Actions

Introduce different resources in her play routine which will build on her experiences e.g. different building resources to knock down when she pushes over the bin. Observe her responses to individual resources – does she show a preference?

Use simple phrases to describe when she is communicating a need or preference e.g. when Suki places the educator's hand on the door handle say 'outside, you want to go outside'. Affirm and validate Suki's communication.

FIGURE 5.4 An example page from Suki's Reflection Toolkit.

In the meeting, we were able to discuss and consider the ways that Suki demonstrated the characteristics of effective learning.

Figures 5.3, 5.4 and 5.5 show how we used the Reflection Toolkit together to consider how we could best support Suki moving forward.

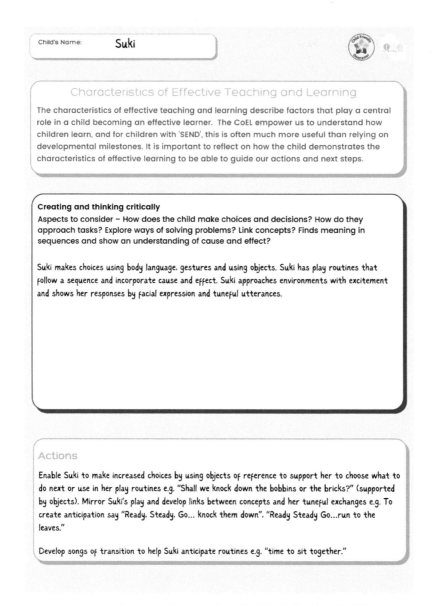

FIGURE 5.5 An example page from Suki's Reflection Toolkit.

Thought Provocations

- Are you able to easily identify the characteristics of effective teaching and learning in your workplace?
- Is co-regulation a high priority in your setting or school?

References

Brooker, L. and Woodhed, M. (eds) (2008) *Developing Positive Identities*. Milton Keynes: The Open University.

Carpenter, B. (2011) Engagement Profile and Scale. The Specialist Schools and Academies Trust (SSAT). http://complexneeds.org.uk/modules/Module-3.2-Engaging-in-learning-key-approaches/All/downloads/m10p040c/engagement_chart_scale_guidance.pdf

Early Years Coalition (2021) Birth to 5 Matters. https://birthto5matters.org.uk/wp-content/uploads/2021/03/Birthto5Matters-download.pdf

Farah, W. (2023) A Beginner's Guide to Intersectionality in the Early Years. Tapestry. https://tapestry.info/a-beginners-guide-to-intersectionality.html

Moylett, H. and Stewart, N. (2012) Development Matters in the Early Years Foundation Stage (EYFS). Early Education. https://dera.ioe.ac.uk/id/eprint/14042/7/development%20matters%20in%20the%20early%20years%20foundation%20stage_Redacted.pdf

Murphy, K. (2022) *A Guide to SEND In the Early Years*. Bloomsbury Publishing.

Stewart, N. (2011) *How Children Learn: The Characteristics of Effective Early Learning*. British Association for Early Childhood Education.

Child's Name

Characteristics of Effective Teaching and Learning

The characteristics of effective teaching and learning describe factors that play a central role in a child becoming an effective learner. They empower us to understand how children learn, and for children with 'SEND', this is often much more useful than relying on developmental milestones. It is important to reflect on how the child demonstrates the CoETL to be able to guide our actions and next steps.

Playing and Exploring

Aspects to consider: Does the child have special or intense interests? Does the child engage in any repeated forms of play? Which areas of the environment is the child drawn to?

Actions

Copyright material from Ann Lowe and Stephen Kilgour (2025), *The Inclusive Early Years Educator*, Routledge

Child's Name

Characteristics of Effective Teaching and Learning

The characteristics of effective teaching and learning describe factors that play a central role in a child becoming an effective learner. They empower us to understand how children learn, and for children with 'SEND', this is often much more useful than relying on developmental milestones. It is important to reflect on how the child demonstrates the CoETL to be able to guide our actions and next steps.

Active Learning

Aspects to consider: What is the child's motivation? How do they persist when faced with challenge? Do they show satisfaction at meeting their own goals? How do they show concentration and engagement?

Actions

Copyright material from Ann Lowe and Stephen Kilgour (2025), *The Inclusive Early Years Educator*, Routledge

Child's Name

Characteristics of Effective Teaching and Learning

The characteristics of effective teaching and learning describe factors that play a central role in a child becoming an effective learner. They empower us to understand how children learn, and for children with 'SEND', this is often much more useful than relying on developmental milestones. It is important to reflect on how the child demonstrates the CoETL to be able to guide our actions and next steps.

Creating and Thinking Critically

Aspects to consider: How does the child make choices and decisions? How do they approach tasks? Explore ways of solving problems? Link concepts? Find meaning in sequences and show an understanding of cause and effect?

Actions

Copyright material from Ann Lowe and Stephen Kilgour (2025), *The Inclusive Early Years Educator*, Routledge

Chapter 6

COMMUNICATION

The ability to communicate is hugely important in everyday life. It could be basic things like letting someone know your choice in a café, or informing a person that you would like to get past them on the bus. In a work environment, it may be explaining a process to a colleague or employee. On a deeper level, the ability to communicate can help us to connect with our loved ones and explain how we are feeling. The majority of us are able to take our communication skills for granted, safe in the knowledge that those in our various social circles will understand us when we need to tell them something. How would it feel, however, if we were faced with a scenario where this wasn't the case?

A common communication challenge for neurotypical adults might be a trip abroad where our home language is not widely spoken. Generally, in situations like ordering food or drink, we can use prompts such as menus to help us to indicate our preferences – especially if photographs are included. Frustration can arise when faced with less common situations such as the need for directions or medical assistance. At these times, we might use gestures or signs to help explain to the other person.

We may feel more extreme feelings of frustration or anxiety if we are unable to contact someone to communicate important or critical information to them – such as when a phone battery is out of charge or being in a place with no signal.

Reflecting on the importance of the ability to communicate effectively, and what it can feel like not being able to, means we are in a better position to understand how central this is for the children in our care.

Types of Communication
Verbal

Spoken language is the most obvious way that the majority of humans communicate their preferences and needs. A powerful aspect of spoken language is that the

DOI: 10.4324/9781003409618-7

communicator can add emphasis or restraint through intonation. In our neurotypical world, verbal communication is generally regarded as the gold standard. As educators or parents, more often than not, we strive for our children to be able to communicate using spoken language and celebrate enthusiastically when progress is made towards this goal. Consider the excitement we demonstrate when we hear a toddler pronounce their first word. However, as inclusive educators, we must also value alternative forms of effective communication. We should not discount the quality of these modes.

Non-Speaking

Non-speaking communication covers a huge range, whether it be subtle elements like the clothes that you are wearing or the way that you sit, to more overt methods like facial expression or gesture. Typically, humans are able to tell another person a lot about the way they're feeling using these signals. A subtle eye roll in a staff meeting at work or an impulsively joyous smile in response to a magical moment. We might throw our arms up in disgust in the direction of a referee at a football match or drop our head when something doesn't go our way. In young children who don't communicate verbally, reaching towards a biscuit tin to let us know they are hungry and pulling at a nappy when wet/dirty are ways that clearly tell us what is required. As inclusive educators, it is vital that we accept gesture as a valid form of communication. It isn't fair to ignore a request that we clearly understand in an effort to sabotage a child's natural mode of communication and force speech – particularly for children who are unable to verbally communicate. We need to validate all children's efforts to communicate.

Written

Some may consider written communication to be slightly old-fashioned, particularly the art of writing a letter. However, many would attest to the fact that things can be easier to communicate effectively on paper or in a text message than verbally. The increase in hi-tech text-to-speech devices means that many people who had previously felt unable to communicate effectively can now live entirely different lives, particularly when used alongside eye-gaze technology. An additional benefit of written communication is that it remains in place as a record of an interaction that we can look back on, whether for clarity or as a reminder of a pleasant interaction. As inclusive educators, we must provide children with opportunities to communicate with us in ways that suit them, which may mean exploring the possibility of using modern technology.

Visual

Visual communication can be very effective and provides an opportunity to be creative. It allows us to convey a message through drawing, symbol or sign. The use of symbols and signing are particularly relevant and powerful when working in specialist learning environments. Improvements in technology have provided educators with resources like 'symbol writers' which can quickly support learners' understanding. An example is a 'chat board' made up of a series of symbols that are relevant to a particular routine or activity. The board provides the educator with an opportunity to reinforce expectations as well as engage in conversation, while allowing the child to do the same. Visual timetables in early years settings are also increasingly popular. These are generally a line of symbols that indicate the order in which things are happening over a period of time (e.g. play, snack, hall). As inclusive educators, we need to ensure that we are providing appropriate visual support in our environments, to ensure that our children have the best chance of understanding expectations and routines.

Listening

Our ability to actively listen is central to truly engaging with another person. This isn't necessarily a straightforward skill, especially given the busy nature of our lives and the seemingly unlimited technological distractions on offer. Listening is generally a two-way process. As we have mentioned previously, being able to 'tune in' to a child is crucially important if we are to be effective educators. Observing and listening are key factors, and if we are working with children with complex support needs, we must be alert to the most subtle of responses. A wiggle of a toe or a unique little sound could provide us with incredibly useful information about the way a child 'listens' and responds. As inclusive educators, we must forget everything we thought we knew about communication and allow ourselves to be present with the children in our care – if we can do this, then we are in the best possible position to learn.

Alternative Communication Approaches

The term AAC (Alternative and Augmentative Communication) is used to describe methods of communication that can be used to help people with learning differences or disabilities to communicate with others. These could be used as an alternative to speech or to supplement it. Hopefully, you will be supported by a speech and language therapist when making decisions linked to alternative communication approaches. It is important that you respect the experience and knowledge of therapists, but also professionally challenge suggestions where appropriate, particularly if you feel that an approach isn't neurodiversity-affirming. The use of the Picture Exchange Communication System (PECS), for example, is increasingly being criticised, particularly by the neurodivergent community, for a number of reasons. Research approaches for yourself and decide if they fit with your pedagogy. Here are a few well-known approaches that may be suggested for use in your setting or school:

Intensive Interaction

The concept of Intensive Interaction is based on the interactions that typically take place between a mother or father and a baby in the first 12 months of a child's life. If a baby looks at us, we naturally smile and attempt to prolong the engagement. If a baby makes a cooing sound, we make that sound back. If they then respond further, we continue to copy their sounds in an effort to establish turn taking. These simple and usually unconsidered actions from a parent/carer are hugely important building blocks for future methods of communication. When using Intensive Interaction in an education setting, we are hoping to gain the attention of a child by adjusting our proximity to them and getting down to their level. It could be that you mimic a sound or copy a facial expression. Our aim is to become more interesting to the child and therefore enable back-and-forth communication. It is important to note that this approach, like many, isn't appropriate for every child. Some children may not like having their sounds or gestures mimicked. Having said that, in my experience it can be a valuable approach for building relationships with young children, particularly if they have complex support needs.

Makaton

Makaton is increasingly being used in early years settings across the country. *Something Special* on CBeebies helped to bring the language programme to the mainstream when it began in 2003, and it has increased in popularity ever since. Makaton was developed way back in 1972 when Margaret Walker conducted research which led to the design of the Makaton Core Vocabulary.

One question that is often asked is 'What is the difference between Makaton and Sign Language?' Annette Butler (2018) summarises this well:

> Makaton is designed to be used to support spoken language... Makaton is often used alongside speech to help aid children and adults with communication. It is common for people to eventually stop using signs as their speech develops.

British Sign Language (BSL) is a language with its own structure and grammar and uses hand signs, body language, facial expression and lip patterns. It is the language used by the deaf community in the UK and, as with any spoken language, is constantly evolving.

The signs used in Makaton are taken from Sign Language and, as Sign Language differs from country to country, so does Makaton. However, unlike Sign Language which has regional variations and dialects, the signs for Makaton will be the same throughout the country.

Makaton is a highly portable way of providing an additional 'visual cue' to a child. It is such an effective method that many parents of young babies now attend 'baby sign' classes to enable more effective communication and understanding. This shows that it has value whether children are neurotypical or neurodivergent. The ability to use Makaton signs is a great tool for any child to have, and the most successful settings embed it across the board, not just for children with learning differences.

Communication Books

Communication books can take many forms, but in essence they are a visual cue to support, scaffold or enhance communication. The beauty of these books is that they can be completely bespoke to the individual, and they should be developed with the children's interests in mind – and also evolve over time as interests change and learning takes place.

More often than not, the books are made up of symbols which are organised into categories. There might be a page devoted to food and drink, or a page that contains symbols linked to a particular activity that the child enjoys such as painting.

Usually the symbols on the left-hand page are fairly consistent throughout and may contain starter words/phrases such as 'I want' or 'I like'. The right-hand page would be more focused on the particular area and might contain verbs such as 'run' or 'jump' for a physical development theme. A child could then combine the symbols from the left-hand side and the right-hand side to communicate a choice or preference.

It is very important that the book is individual to the child, not just in terms of interests but also through the use of symbols that represent the child. Good-quality symbol maker programs allow you to alter the skin colour of the people who feature, and they also contain a varied range of food and drink examples.

The success of a communication book usually relies upon the quality of support and modelling from communication partners, as well as consistent use across a child's day, both at home and in their setting or school. As educators, we can reinforce our own messages to a communication book user by pointing at the relevant symbols in the child's book as we speak. The best examples of communication books not only provide opportunities for practical requests/choice making, but also allow for communication opportunities linked to conversations around feelings or opportunities for casual 'chat'.

Educator's View – Simon Wright (Assistant Head Teacher and EYFS Lead, Cherry Garden School, London)

Working in a school where children have a vast range of communication differences, it is important to equip children with a 'voice' that they can use in a functional way and for them to be understood by a range of communication partners.

We try to ensure that each child has an individualised system, working within our approach that each child is an individual and their learning journey will be unique. As children develop their confidence and ability to communicate in different ways (this could be speech, signing, symbols), this opens up their engagements with adults, their peers and the world around them.

Teaching through regular routines can build confidence and understanding, then we generalise to wider contexts and, finally, children use their voice to have a truly child-led experience in school, making choices and engaging in the things that interest them the most.

We know that being able to communicate basic wants and needs, comment or even just have a 'chat' ensures children feel safe and ready to learn. It is essential that children with a communication difference have a way of communicating in a way that works for them and are not diverted down a path that supports them to communicate in the way that society deems to be the norm. Our children are their happiest when they can tell you what it is they want you to know about them.

Language Racism and Oralism

Language racism is a concept we should be familiar with as educators, particularly if we work with families of children from minoritised backgrounds.

Students who are English Language Learners may face discrimination because of their limited English proficiency. Teachers may assume they are less intelligent or less capable than their peers who speak 'English fluently'. Students who may not speak 'standardised English' also face discrimination as teachers may assume that the way they speak is 'broken, slang, informal'.

(Farah, 2023, p.11)

It is important as inclusive educators that we value and embrace all forms of spoken language, as opposed to believing that traditional English should be the 'end-goal' for all communicators.

In addition, we must be aware that *spoken* English should not always be the ultimate aim for all communicators. Many deaf people have spoken out over the issue of 'oralism' in teaching. To be 'oralist' is to favour spoken language over manual methods, upholding the idea that speech is the best method of communication. As inclusive educators, we should challenge this notion and allow ourselves to be open to a range of communication approaches while withholding judgement as to the 'best'. As always, we must centre the child in our decision making.

Developing a Reflective Approach to Inclusive Communication Practice in Doncaster
Reflecting on Verbal and Non-Speaking Communication

South Yorkshire Local Authority areas, including Doncaster, have benefitted from additional funding to support children's communication and language skills over recent years due to stark figures from research into the 2018 Foundation Stage Profile results that indicated that many children in South Yorkshire did not achieve the expected level of development in communication, language and literacy in 2018. This amounts to 4,650, equivalent to approximately 30 per cent of children in South Yorkshire.

However, there is much debate as to whether the Early Years Foundation Stage Profile measure of attainment is appropriate for neurodivergent children. There have been a number of benefits to the additional funding, enabling an enhancement of services available for families, as well as professional development opportunities for the early years workforce, dedicated to developing verbal communication for all children.

One of these benefits has been the creation of South Yorkshire Talking Together, a regional initiative to support children's speech, language and communication development. The four local authorities in the region (Barnsley, Rotherham, Doncaster and Sheffield) teamed up with South Yorkshire Futures – Sheffield Hallam University's social mobility partnership – to support children to develop verbal communication skills.

A range of programmes have then emerged from this initiative, allowing opportunities for a wide range of support for parents, carers, practitioners, and anyone else working or interacting with children under the age of 5, to learn and share key messages that support early speech, language and communication development. Services that have been established as part of the project include Talking Together and Growing Talk. These are two programmes which enable enhanced communication practitioners to work with a family on early communication skills over a period of months, developing a toolkit to support their child's communication skills. This could be within a playgroup provision or at home over a series of visits. These family services were developed in Doncaster Local Authority.

The additional funding from the project has enabled the South Yorkshire early years sector to learn more about different aspects of communication and the importance of valuing all methods of communication, not considering speech to be superior to other forms.

This emphasis on inclusivity as opposed to oralist approaches was demonstrated at the recent Doncaster Improving Early Years Outcomes Conference. I was asked to speak as part of a panel of experts in the field of early years including Ruth Churchill Dower, a doctoral researcher at Manchester Metropolitan University, author of *Creativity and the Arts in Early Childhood: Supporting Young Children's Development and Wellbeing* and founder of Earlyarts. Ruth spoke passionately about the work she does to develop communication through movement and the arts. She referred to the many neurodivergent children she works with who have a wealth of communication skills which are primarily non-speaking but valid ways to express thoughts and feelings.

All children (and adults, for that matter) express themselves in different (multimodal and multisensory) ways which are influenced by their cultural, social and economic histories, their likes and dislikes, age, gender and numerous other factors. For instance, consider your new intake coming into an unfamiliar space on their first day of term. Some children like to twirl, skip or jump around to 'map it out' with their bodies. Others like to peek out from behind a parent's leg while taking in the environment and atmosphere, mapping it out with their eyes. Others still might scoot to the reading corner touching the books, feeling the shapes and textures of props that will bring stories to life, mapping the space with all of their senses. These responses are all different, and all wonderful ways of expressing their relationships with the world around them.

Since the demands of early years teaching and learning tend to prioritise language, sadly we miss so much of how young children's bodies, senses and ideas express themselves. Odd refrains that are repeatedly hummed, unusual noises made to experiment with the sensations inside the mouth, little skips or dances or other gestures children make while playing... Far from being 'uncommunicative' or 'inexpressive', these are all important ways of learning that young children show us when we take time to listen to their bodies and senses with our bodies and senses. It's all about experimenting with being rather than doing.

I have experienced the transformation in settings where an educator has stopped talking and instead offered a little hand-dance to a child's made-up song, or started humming in time to a child's rocking, or gently chalked a child's twirls and squirls as they move across the playground, holding on to this relief from words for as long as possible. The educator has recognised the power of the spaces in between (or beyond) words to invite new experiences and ideas, and that this often starts with movement – a universal body language. Children seem to inhabit these spaces more easily, and it is here where the anxieties and expectations of having to speak can fall away. Different modes of expression find a warm welcome in these spaces, become enjoyed and experimented with and, on many occasions, lead to squeals of delight and verbal articulations of one sort or another.

Not-speaking is incredibly valuable. It helps us become more attuned to the unspoken messages about the need for speech that bombard us every day, creating blocks for children whose senses and bodies need to express themselves differently. It sounds easy to create spaces for not-speaking. But it is actually quite difficult because verbal language is so embedded into the fabric of daily life. Try it and see how things change! You'll be amazed how surprising, interesting and relaxing it is for both adults and children once the unfamiliarity of not-speaking melts away. Until, that is, your non-speaking children find they have plenty to say!

Ruth Churchill Dower (Doctoral Researcher at
Manchester Metropolitan University)

I spoke to my colleague Alison Fleetwood, who organised the event and who has led the South Yorkshire Talking Together project from its conception. Alison commented on her insight following the panel's contributions. She drew on the nurture approach and importance of connections and was keen to embed the notion of communication through movement into the Talking Together Training for early years educators. Since the conference, I have had many conversations with practitioners who attended about the ways they are beginning to reflect on their practice to value all communication.

> When I started developing the Talking Together Pathway for Doncaster, I felt very strongly about the need to triangulate the offer to ensure support for professionals, parents and children. In doing this, we have been able to spread consistent messages throughout our workforce and communities about how 53 per cent of communication is non-verbal. Through attunement with the child and the creation of a communication-friendly culture we can support all children to understand, to be understood and to thrive.
>
> Alison Fleetwood (Service Manager Family Hubs,
> Early Years and Talking Together)

A beneficial addition to the Early Years Inclusion Team through the initiative has been a speech and language therapist and a dedicated team of communication specialists. As a team, they have been able to deliver training for early years practitioners on communication strategies, upskilling the early years workforce in Doncaster. Becky Massey (Speech and Language Therapist) describes some of feedback from the training:

> We have two modules available for professionals working within the early years to attend, and both focus on all aspects of communication, not just spoken language, and how these skills can be nurtured and supported within our young children. One of the first things we discuss is the difference between speech, language and communication, and professionals report feeling more confident following our training in understanding the difference between these three terms and recognising the different ways in which a child can communicate without the need for spoken language. There is an activity where the group have to order themselves alphabetically without talking and it always promotes lots

of discussion afterwards about all the different ways they were able to share a message without words. A confidence rating scale is taken before and after the session which increases for the majority of individuals. One delegate in particular has been very forthcoming with how they have used the training in their everyday practice and provided examples of nurturing rich communication opportunities for all children within their care at varying levels of communication ability.

Becky Massey (Talking Together Speech Therapist)

Reflecting on Written Communication – A Case Study

Filip had been referred to the Early Years Inclusion Team in Doncaster by a setting in the south of Doncaster in Autumn 2022 when he had been attending the setting for a few months. The nursery had observed that Filip's development was diverging from the typical developmental pathway. They had requested some advice to develop their techniques in helping him to further his communication and social skills, as well as how to support him to keep safe in the setting by supporting his receptive language. Filip attended the nursery setting 8am–6pm every day. I visited him in the spring term to get to know him better and worked alongside his key worker to learn more about his communication.

My first observation about Filip was the relationship he had with his key worker. He had a bond with Clair which demonstrated a deep connection. Clair was attuned to his needs and had a wealth of knowledge about his interests, sensory-seeking behaviours and abilities. Clair was keen to talk to me about Filip's strengths and the unique way he responded to written letters, symbols and numbers. Clair had observed that Filip had a keen interest in numbers. He could name many numbers and letters. He enjoyed looking at written symbols and attempting to write or copy the symbols himself. His verbal communication was most evident when he named letters of the alphabet, and he would prompt Clair to draw letters and numbers by leading her to the chalk board and placing his hand on hers. Filip also showed a love of shapes and was intrinsically motivated to find his favourite shape puzzle, sometimes attempting to seek it from a high shelf or cupboard. Filip would look at pictures and books, showing inquisitiveness about written forms.

Clair had found that transition times were challenging for her to support Filip to move to the table or sit for snack time or group time. We discussed devising some social stories with visuals to help Filip to understand what would happen during a particular part of the day. When writing the social stories, it was important to consider how to support Filip to prepare for each experience (i.e. what, where, duration, who?) and the reason for doing it. We devised some pages together for simple routines and decided to use photographs to help with understanding:

At 10 am we have snack time (picture of fruit on a plate and clock saying '10 am').
It lasts for 3 minutes (picture of the egg timer saying '3 minutes').
You can sit at the table with your friends (photograph with Filip and friends at the table).
You can have your shape sorter with you (photograph of shape sorter alongside snack).
Eating snack keeps you healthy (photograph of Filip eating).

Clair was keen to try the social stories and support Filip's understanding of routines help him to feel secure to eat snack at nursery.

Reflecting on Visual Communication

Visual supports are integral to much of the work we do with early years settings in Doncaster. Not only are they useful for neurodivergent children, but they are also effective with neurotypical children in helping them to understand instructions, predict routines, remember ways to keep themselves safe and encourage independence.

I completed the Enhanced Level training in Makaton 12 years ago and since then I have used it daily in my practice to develop expressive communication and support understanding. I have found it to be a lifeline for helping to reduce frustration and increase confidence for children.

The benefits of Makaton were most recently highlighted when I led an Introduction to Makaton session for parents who were currently receiving support from the Doncaster Portage Service. Portage Home Visitor, Sarah McMahon, was working with a family in the east of Doncaster. Sarah had talked to parents about the benefits of using Makaton and had modelled the use of key signs on weekly home visits. The family had really taken on board the aspects of Makaton aiding their child's communication and had started to model the signs at home with their child. Mum described the signs she had used and modelled and how she had noticed that her child was beginning to use Makaton to sign to her. This had developed the child's listening and attention skills and increased the child's level of engagement.

Sarah describes the benefits of using Makaton as a Portage Home Visitor:

> Makaton is a widely used alternative form of communication that supports children who may be pre-verbal or unable to express their wants and needs through speech. Within my role as Portage Home Visitor, I use Makaton daily within my home visits and group settings. I feel there are a number of benefits of using Makaton – it enables children to make choices and have a voice, and it gives them autonomy to express themselves. For example, a child who I support is pre-verbal and has a diagnosis of cerebral palsy. I introduced Makaton and have consistently used the sign 'more' during play sessions. The child's parents have also used it within the daily routine and mealtimes, and the first time the child signed back 'more' was such a significant moment. Without Makaton, there would be an additional barrier for children who are pre-verbal; this then increases frustration for the child and parent and takes away the child's own voice. Another example of the benefit of Makaton is when signing nursery rhymes. Children can indicate what song they would like and through repetition can begin to join in with the signs to their favourite nursery rhyme.
>
> Sarah McMahon (Portage Home Visitor)

Makaton can be beneficial for all children, not only neurodivergent children. The signs help children to understand key concepts and words when the meaning of verbal language can be lost, due to fast-paced instructions and noisy environments in early years settings. We have regular requests from schools and early years setting to deliver introductory Makaton sessions, training over 100 educators most terms in Doncaster.

Developing Intensive Interaction in Doncaster

We were fortunate to receive Intensive Interaction training from Doncaster Education Psychologist Laura De Cabo Seron at a recent SENCO Cluster. My colleague Mandy Haddock had arranged for Laura to deliver a session on the approach for SENCOs in Doncaster to enhance their professional development in the area of communication.

Laura describes Intensive Interaction below:

> Intensive Interaction is a person-centred communication approach that prioritises the establishment of emotional and social connections. It is adaptable to the unique needs of each child, and it will look different every time we implement it, and it should be tailored to every child we deliver it to. It is a one-to-one intervention that can be implemented spontaneously during daily routines and should involve positive, welcoming body language to convey interest and support.
>
> Intensive Interaction should be used whenever there is an opportunity to foster communication. It promotes communication by offering experiences of attunement and cause/effect type of interactions with the key adult. It will enable the child to feel more included, have an improved quality of life and strengthen their relationship with the adult delivering this intervention.
>
> Intensive Interaction should always start with a close observation and listening period with the child, in order to identify their communication cues and behaviour. It is very important that this intervention is delivered by adults who know the child well and are attuned. When implementing this intervention, it is important to track their progress by monitoring the frequency of repeated activities, the expansion of the repertoire of responses, the transition of interactions from unintentional to intentional and any emotional responses we may observe (e.g. smiling).
>
> Laura De Cabo Seron (Educational Psychologist at Doncaster Council)

Since the session, I have observed many settings using the approach to tune in to children's authentic play, resulting in increased instances of two-way communication.

Reflecting on Intensive Interaction – A Case Study

A setting in the north of Doncaster had referred a child, Maryam, to the Early Years Inclusion Team. They had observed that Maryam's communication was developing differently to her neurotypical peers and asked for some support with strategies to increase communication. On my visit to observe Maryam, I modelled some Intensive Interaction techniques. At first, this involved watching and looking for signs of communication: a moment of eye contact with myself and then eye gaze towards a small world figure she was playing with; facial expressions while playing with the figures; smiles as she moved the small world princesses up and down the concrete path. Initially, I mirrored some of her play and moved alongside her in the outdoor area, positioning myself as the learner. I used open body language and spoke to the practitioners about positioning ourselves as learners. This was particularly significant in supporting the educators to embrace new strategies.

Following lots of tuning in and mirroring Maryam, I began to try to create moments of turn taking and build anticipation by joining her play. For example, I used the princess figures to model jumping, following her gesturing moving the figure up and down. I said, 'Princess is jumping fast!' while mirroring Maryam's play. I noticed that Maryam responded by smiling, and when I stopped the princess jumping, Maryam made some brief eye contact with me. I then carried on with 'jump again' and continued to make the princess jump. This led into a number of moments of anticipation and also turn taking as Maryam started to jump with her princess too. I began to build some rhyme and melody into the interactions. The educators had observed Maryam's favourite song was 'Round and Round the Garden'; I recommended adapting this song to various play-based situations (e.g. Round and Round the Princess). The aim was to increase enjoyment in rhythm and rhyme, thereby increasing communication. I led a staff meeting on Intensive Interaction to advise how to embed the approach. The educators were particularly keen to develop their knowledge and their practice to value Mayam's body language, gestures, expressions and eye gaze as key aspects of her communication.

Reflecting on Language Racism and Oralism in Doncaster

Doncaster is a growing, diverse place with a range of cultures and languages spoken. Many of our early years providers are continually reviewing and improving how they foster a sense of belonging and encourage children to communicate in their first language, reflecting on the benefits of all communication for all children in the setting.

It is important to acknowledge that we are on a journey of improvement to raise awareness of language racism. Many providers in Doncaster are becoming more aware of the discrimination faced when spoken English is upheld as an ideal, and are changing the ways they embrace and value other spoken languages.

During network events, providers have been invited to share good practice, particularly in relation to how we develop representation of different languages within provision and on admission. Reflecting collectively and sharing ideas has so many benefits. At a recent CPD session, we discussed the benefits of learning key words in a child's home language. This not only supports understanding but enables a child to feel increasingly secure in a setting. Talking to parents when a child joins a setting about routines and key words can be especially beneficial to support a child's access to care routines such as toileting and food. Books, stories, rhymes and greetings are great starting points for promoting different languages and beginning the journey to anti-racist practice.

Thought Provocations

- Is there an understanding in your setting of the range of ways that a child can communicate?
- Is your practice biased towards spoken language?

References

Butler, A. (2018) What's the difference between BSL and Makaton? Primary Sign Language. www
.primarysign.co.uk/index.php?/announcement/2-what%E2%80%99s-the-difference-between-bsl
-and-makaton
Farah, W. (2023) A Beginner's Guide to Intersectionality in the Early Years. Tapestry. https://tapestry
.info/a-beginners-guide-to-intersectionality.html

Child's Name

Communication

Communication skills are important to children's development. Neurodivergent children may develop their communication skills in different ways – it is important to celebrate and reflect upon the individual child's communication journey and notice the steps of progression each individual child is making on their own pathway. The development of children's communication underpins all seven areas of learning and development in the EYFS. Use the space below to reflect and comment on how the child is showing communication skills. Consider whether the child:

- Demonstrates communication intent – e.g. vocalising sounds, pointing or shifting eye gaze.
- Communicates their enjoyment of rhyme or rhythmic activities.
- Understands simple commands in context – e.g. 'pick it up', 'get your coat'.
- Demonstrates understanding of vocabulary related to familiar people and common objects.
- Is developing speech sounds (p, b, t, d, n, m, initially).
- Chatters or babbles using range of different sounds and intonation. Attempts to imitate new words. Has a vocabulary of words or signs or visual representations used meaningfully.

Actions

Copyright material from Ann Lowe and Stephen Kilgour (2025), *The Inclusive Early Years Educator*, Routledge

Chapter 7

PLAY

Unsurprisingly, play and engagement are recurring themes in a book for early years educators. It is always worth reiterating, however, the importance of truly valuing our children's play.

Play is lifelong – even if we don't necessarily consider ourselves to be genuinely playing as adults. It's not unusual for a group of 40-somethings to have a game of five-a-side football each week, or to enjoy a bingo night, for an adult to become engrossed in 'tinkering' with a creative project. It is all play, and the beauty of play is that we don't always know what the outcome will be. Will your team win or lose their game? Will that bench you're making out of old bits of wood balance or be endearingly wobbly? One aspect of play that doesn't change is the fact that we keep learning. The realisation that your opponent on the pitch always shoots when they're on their left foot, or that a particular saw cuts more precisely with a certain shaped piece of wood. Even tasks that may seem mundane involve us experimenting and playing with different ideas – cooking an evening meal and changing a recipe slightly by adding an extra ingredient can go either way, but we certainly learn from the experience – maybe chocolate in the chilli was a step too far!

Thankfully, in the early years the vast majority of settings and schools do value the power of play as a vehicle for learning. There is, however, constant pressure from policy makers to add a level of formality to the learning experience for our youngest children. In some cases, this can result in things like extended phonics sessions on the carpet in nursery or worksheets in Reception, as well as an increase in teacher-directed time or 'intervention' groups. It is unfortunate that 'preparation for school' can sometimes overtake supportive individual child development as the main goal for many in the early years. This pressure can be particularly strong in Reception classes, especially when senior leadership teams in primary schools often don't have any EYFS experience. Add to this the pressure of outside agencies making judgements about the quality of progress across a school, and we have the perfect storm for forgetting the basics of early childhood education.

DOI: 10.4324/9781003409618-8

That is not to say that early years educators don't try to push back against this rhetoric, but it can be extremely challenging, particularly if a Reception teacher is a lone voice in a school. Since the reforms in the early years, which had the intention of doing away with data-focused assessment, there are still frequent stories on social media of headteachers who remain convinced that 'data drops' for the youngest children in their school are still necessary. It is understandable why. Headteachers are accountable, and data is the simplest way for them to demonstrate progress/quality to people who are asking difficult questions. Whether it be school governors, the local authority, or Ofsted, the quickest way to satisfy their requests for information is to show them some numbers. The positive news is that Ofsted have said that they will no longer ask to see progress data – so hopefully, one day, it will genuinely be a thing of the past.

Schematic Play

Piaget (1952, p.7) defined a schema as 'a cohesive, repeatable action sequence possessing component actions that are tightly interconnected and governed by a core meaning'. In simpler terms, Cathy Nutbrown (2006, p. 7) explains schema as 'a way of labelling children's consistent patterns of action'. The thinking is that if educators can observe and interpret these patterns, then they are in a better position to provide children with situations in which they can learn more effectively.

PACEY (the Professional Association for Childcare and Early Years) define nine of the most common schema as follows:

- **Trajectory** – creating lines in space by climbing up and jumping down. Dropping items from up high.
- **Positioning** – lining items up and putting them in groups.
- **Enveloping** – covering themselves or objects completely. Wrapping items up or placing them in containers.
- **Rotating** – enjoys spinning items round and round. Likes to run around in circles or being swung round.
- **Enclosing** – adding boundaries to play areas e.g. fences around animals. Adding borders to pictures.
- **Transporting** – carrying or moving items from one place to another; carrying items in containers or bags.
- **Connecting** – setting out and dismantling tracks, constructing, joining items together with tape or glue.

- **Transforming** – exploring the changing states of materials, transforming them from a solid to liquid state and back again.
- **Orienteering** – an interest in positioning themselves or objects in different places or positions e.g. upside down or on their side.

(PACEY, 2024)

It is sometimes the case that we can get too caught up in a child's interest, particularly if we are working with a neurodivergent child. If, for example, the child loves playing with cars, we might be inclined to go on the hunt for car-themed activities to engage them in other areas of the learning environment. This could work, but it would also be useful to think on a deeper level about what it is they are actually doing with the cars. Is it the pushing of the cars or seeing the wheels spin that is actually causing the interest? A child who is interested in trains might actually be particularly interested in the way that they connect together or line up rather than the more general theme. Considering schema is a helpful addition to our observational toolkit, but as inclusive educators, we need to remember that all children are unique, and individual children's play won't necessarily fit neatly into the schema definitions provided.

Play Progression

In typically developing children, the progression of play skills tends to follow a familiar pattern. As early years educators, it is useful to have an awareness of these developmental stages, so that expectations are appropriate, and environments can be set up in a way that is most likely to meet the needs of the group.

The following play milestones were collated/created for Cherry Garden School as part of their Branch Map assessment framework. As with any child development discussions, this isn't an exact science, but the information can be helpful when planning provision. The intention of these milestones is not to gather assessment data, but to enable discussions. There is no expectation that children will develop along typical pathways, particularly if they have learning differences or a disability. *This is crucially important to note.*

Birth to 5 months
Laughs in response to playful interactions
Responds to a range of stimuli
5–10 months
Takes part in and enjoys back-and-forth vocal interactions
Starts to enjoy peek-a-boo style games

Manipulates and explores materials and objects
10–15 months
Interacts with toys that move, bend or make a noise
Plays with items in different ways: pulls, pushes, squeezes, bangs
Exploration of cause-and-effect toys becomes more complex – twisting, turning, on and off
15–22 months
Starts to engage in functional play – puts a hat on, uses a spoon with a bowl, pushes a car, etc.
Explores filling and emptying containers
Takes part in solitary play – completing puzzles, building with blocks, etc.
More interested in physical play – sliding, swinging, climbing
Engages with sorting toys like shape boxes and stacking rings
Takes part in more 'pretend play' – cooking, feeding the baby, driving the toy car
22–29 months
Sequences actions together – puts people inside a vehicle, then pushes it along the floor
Plays alongside other children, but not necessarily with them (parallel play)
Pretend play becomes more abstract – a block can become a phone, a box can be a car, etc.
Uses construction materials to create their own simple structures and arrangements
29–36 months
Gross motor skills improving so they can enjoy tricycles and throwing games
Begins to take turns with 2–3 other children in play
Takes part in pretend play that involves others
36–48 months
Can kick a ball towards a target more accurately and understands that some games have a purpose
Develops 'associate play' – increasing the amount of interaction with other children in play
Children become more interested in the concept of becoming 'friends'
Participates in 'group play' – singing and dancing games, art activities, etc.
48–60 months
Play becomes increasingly 'co-operative' with other children who engage with each other as well as with the activity
Peer relationships continue to develop through play and children begin to forge stronger friendships

Neurodivergent Play

One of the issues with resources or guidance that detail milestones you may expect to find in typically developing children (like the play progression information above) is that some educators become too focused on these pathways. There is also a risk of the milestones listed becoming 'targets' that are given significant worth for all children. This is not to say that knowledge of child development isn't important for those working in settings or schools, but there also needs to be flexibility in our thinking! Not all children progress in exactly the same way (very few actually do). For example, a child's route to confident independent walking will rarely line up neatly with a peer. Often progression looks broadly the same, but occasionally children miss out crawling altogether, while ultimately still reach the same endpoint.

If we place too much value on typical developmental milestones for children with learning differences or disabilities, we risk undermining the progress they may be showing in other ways. When it comes to play, it can be the case that educators become judgemental about the quality of a child's play skills. The gold standard of co-operative, imaginative, 'purposeful' play in the home corner can skew our ability to place value on the play of children who are exploring and learning in different ways.

The play patterns and cultures of neurodivergent and disabled children are often misunderstood because research has historically focused on proving that neurodivergent play is a problem to be fixed. Therefore, children with development differences must be taught how to play properly, functionally or appropriately – or, in short, to play, learn and behave more like their neurotypical peers. When a child's play 'looks' different to what we usually observe, there can be a tendency to see this as evidence that their play is trivial, pointless or lacks value (Murphy, 2023, p.3).

In the early years, we are encouraged to provide opportunities for 'open-ended' play. If we are truly doing this, then we shouldn't be concerned if a child's play takes them in a direction that we are unfamiliar or uncomfortable with (providing everyone is safe). It is important that we ourselves are open to learning more about styles of play and understand the value of that play for an individual child.

Educator's View – Kerry Murphy, Neurodiversity and Early Childhood Specialist

Here are three strategies for empowering play for children with learning differences:

Make time for self-directed pure play

As an educator, you can advocate for an environment that enables uninterrupted time for self-directed pure play and commit to withholding judgements or prior misconceptions about that play. Within that uninterrupted time, your observational attention and attunement is crucial in making sense of that play. With neurodivergent children, it might be that things don't make sense for a while. That is okay. Remember Trawick's words – 'play is intentionally ambiguous'. If everything was so obvious, would it invite as much curiosity? One tool you may find useful is to use a Play Dictionary to look for patterns in play._

Affirm rather than deny interests

As a child, I related more to objects than people, often called object personification. I personified every little thing, and every little thing had feelings. Ornaments delighted me as I imagined scenarios in my head of their adventures when the humans left the room. I could daydream for hours. I was too solitary and 'in my own head' to the outsider. Yet it was when I felt most happy. I liked playing 'alone' although I collected 'creatures' and would meticulously line them up on my bed every morning, and so I never envisioned myself as being alone. I just preferred plushies to other kids. I still prefer plushies to humans, which often leads to people thinking of me as childish and child-like (an insult often directed at autistic people – yet I only ever receive it as a compliment). Our interests in early childhood contribute to who we are as individuals. Rather than judging or re-directing, we must figure out why they mean so much to the child or children we care for.

Reframe language

Take time to notice how you speak about neurodivergent children's play. For example, do you talk about their play skills as symptoms of their neurotype. 'They just spin around all day because they are autistic' as opposed to 'They seem to be doing spinning stims. I wonder what motivates that interest? Is it rotational? Is it soothing? Does it replicate something they have seen? Could I join in and connect with that play pattern?'

You can download Kerry's Beginner's Guide to Self-Directed Neurodivergent Play by scanning Figure 7.1.

FIGURE 7.1 A QR code linking to the Beginner's Guide to Self-Directed Neurodivergent Play

Developing a Reflective Approach to Neurodivergent Play in Doncaster

We were keen to develop our understanding of neurodiversity-affirming practice in Doncaster and invited Kerry Murphy to present at our Essential Knowledge Briefing meeting for early years educators in spring 2022. Kerry spoke passionately about the importance of giving value to all play: positioning ourselves as learners, to be curious about a child's play without the barriers and constraints of assumptions about how resources 'should' be played with, or what typical play with them looks like.

This sparked reflection for educators in Doncaster, particularly about the way they had previously scaffolded play. Kerry's perspective really flipped thinking for many of us in the team. We had often been setting expectations that a child would reach play outcomes or play with a resource with purpose, building up their skills in one direction (e.g. using bricks to build a tower). It provoked a range of questions. Had our preoccupation with sticking to the traditional purpose of a resource resulted in us missing opportunities to support a child to develop their play in a variety of ways? Had the use of typically developing play as our guide capped many learning and play opportunities, by trying to change neurodivergent play into neurotypical play?

Since then, there has been a shift in our team and in Doncaster early years settings to encourage a child's autonomy in play and value all play in its purest form.

Reflecting on Neurodivergent Play – A Case Study

Nolan attended a nursery in the north of Doncaster and had been referred to the Early Years Inclusion Team for some advice to develop his learning.

I observed Nolan exploring the indoor environment in the foundation unit. Nolan was accessing the small world area and the building bricks. I watched him closely in his play. Nolan was absorbed in his own child-initiated activity, enclosing small world animals and figures using blocks. He had made a number of squares and triangles on a carpet area and had placed an animal inside each enclosed space. Nolan continued to build shapes to enclose the animals until he reached around 15 animals and then he accessed a box of pebbles and placed a pebble in each enclosed space with an animal. Nolan used some single words to name the animals.

Later on during the session, Nolan accessed the outside area. I observed that he showed most enjoyment in the tunnel area under the climbing equipment. He placed himself inside the tunnel on his back with his feet on the roof of the tunnel. His key worker commented how he often spent lots of time in the tunnel and that it could sometimes be a challenge to motivate him to come out. Nolan's other favourite space outside was the crate area. He enjoyed placing items underneath the crates or making a square with the crates and planks and placing items in the middle.

I spoke to the educators and Nolan's parents about his interests and behaviours. Nolan seemed to be developing an enclosure schema, adding boundaries or borders within much of his play. We discussed the ways that we could develop play around this schema and offered Nolan an extended range of resources to continue to develop his schematic play. We discussed language and single words that could be developed including using prepositions such as 'inside', 'on' and 'next to' to further develop his understanding and use of three key words. We also discussed the ways we could focus outcomes on skills such as developing fine motor skills, developing counting vocabulary and developing language through enabling access to child-directed play and Intensive Interaction.

By reflecting on Nolan's schematic play to plan our next steps of support, we were able to uphold his authentic play.

Reflecting on Neurodivergent Play – A Case Study

Jan began attending a childminding setting in the north of Doncaster. Sarah, Jan's childminder, had referred Jan to the Early Years Inclusion Team for advice as she felt he wasn't meeting typically developing milestones. I visited Jan in Sarah's home, observing him and playing alongside. Sarah explained that she had observed that Jan showed a deep interest in spinning objects, circles and hoops. She had collected a range of resources to engage Jan, including spinning tops, hoop stacking rings and wooden hoops. Jan accessed the resources and showed interest in pushing the wooden hoops across the floor on their side and watching the spinning tops whirl round.

I played alongside Jan, exploring the resources, developing curiosity in my approach and trying to find out more about Jan's interests in play. We observed that Jan enjoyed pushing and pulling the circular objects and decided to introduce a train track and trains set up in a circle shape. I initially played with the train alongside Jan, making 'choo, choo' sounds as I pushed the train around the track. Jan began to show an interest in the trains and picked the vehicles up, turning the wheels with his fingers. Jan spent a few moments exploring these and then showed an interest in the circular train track. Jan briefly used an eye gaze to look at me fleetingly as I pushed a train around the track.

Jan watched the trains going round the track, glancing between the train wheels in between his fingers and the track. After a few minutes, Jan joined me at the train track and watched as I pushed the trains round. When I paused momentarily, Jan began to vocalise and placed the train in my hand. I signed 'more', said 'more' and moved the train around the track. Pausing again, Jan vocalised and pushed my hand on the train. We repeated this exchange a few times, and then Jan continued the play by pushing another train around the track.

We reflected on Jan's play afterwards. Sarah said that although the train track had been available as a play resource before, this was the first time she had seen Jan show an interest in it. We discussed whether it was the circular track, the spinning of the wheels or the pushing of the vehicles that had motivated Jan to become involved. We were still unsure, and to determine Jan's true motivation, we both agreed that Sarah would need to do more observation of Jan's child-initiated play.

We discussed Jan's communication throughout the visit, first identifying the way that Jan showed curiosity in the train track play by looking over briefly towards me and watching the play fleetingly. We discussed how this could be difficult to pick up unless we had intently observed Jan and were looking for very slight indications that he was beginning to show an interest in the play. We discussed using the train in his hand as a starting point to develop engagement, tapping into his interest in circles and pushing as a way to support Jan's exploration of different experiences.

Sarah also observed that during the train track activity, Jan showed increased verbal communication. Jan had indicated by verbal communication that he wanted an activity to continue. We discussed strategies to encourage this by pausing during an interaction, waiting to see Jan's responses and following his lead. We discussed how we could use this strategy in many play experiences with Jan. The key recommendation from my visit was to be curious and to position ourselves as a learner in Jan's play.

Reflecting on Neurodivergent Play – A Case Study

Ziva had been referred to the Portage Service due to her social and communication differences and divergent development. Nicky Brettoner (Portage Home Visitor) was working with Ziva and her family to understand more about Ziva's learning and to support opportunities to enable her to make progress.

Nicky observed that Ziva explored resources in different ways to typically developing children. Ziva often enjoyed exploring resources with her whole body, immersing herself in experiences. While visiting Ziva at home, her parents began to discuss aspects of Ziva's play that were becoming more difficult to manage when they attended play groups and early years settings, as Ziva played with provision in very different ways to typically developing children.

The Portage team in Doncaster run their own group, POG (Portage Opportunity Group). Nicky described how in this group they adapt and change resources and provision to meet individual children's needs:

> At POG, when a child plays in the water and wants to get in fully to explore, we pop the water tray on the floor and allow them in (with parent's permission). If they want to explore the paint by sitting in the paint tray, we let them. I love it this way and so do the children and so do the parents. Often in a nursery, I find staff to have lots of expectations of how children should play (water play should be with hands, exploring while standing at the side). I find it's often about having expectations and preparing children for school and having boundaries (instead of valuing play).
>
> Nicky Brettoner (Portage Home Visitor)

Nicky and I discussed the challenges in trying to change the narrative of 'purposeful play' and enabling neurodivergent children's play to be valued and upheld in importance in the same way as typical development styles. We agreed that different professionals are at different stages of their learning, but that using the strategies described by Kerry Murphy – **affirming interests**, **reframing language** and **making time** – we can begin to empower children's neurodivergent play.

Nicky talked with the family about the groups at the family hub they attended, and they agreed to her joining them at a group. Nicky had already established relationships with the family hub facilitators, and prior to the next session, she made contact with them to ask about their observations of Ziva. Nicky explained that the family were finding the sessions challenging at times, as Ziva wanted to explore resources in different ways, and this was causing frustration for Ziva and for Mum during the session. Nicky suggested some changes to provision that could reduce Ziva's frustrations and enable her individual play.

Nicky shared what she had observed about Ziva's learning at home with the facilitators of the group, and how she had enabled Ziva's exploration and play in the POG group by changing some of the ways resources were presented. Nicky supported the facilitators to adapt their provision by offering water provision outside to enable Ziva to fully immerse herself in it, and by offering more resources on the floor rather than table based, allowing Ziva to explore with her full body without climbing on to tables. They were keen to learn more as Nicky explained the benefits of enabling individual, self-directed play in all its forms.

Nicky affirmed Ziva's interests by enhancing the provision, enabling time and space for her to engage in self-directed play. As a result, the group became more accessible to Ziva and her family (and to other children too!). By reframing her thinking and language, Nicky had started a powerful shift in thinking about neurodivergent play and the ways we can empower it. There is still much we can do, but a seed has been planted!

Promoting a Neurodiversity-Affirming Approach in Doncaster

One of the recurring themes that emerges from my meetings with settings is the concern about doing things differently for individual children: 'If we do things differently for them, they'll all want to do that' or 'How do we do things differently for one and not for everyone else?'

In answering this question, I often go back to our core concept as educators: to educate in all forms – typical development or neurodivergent development – our role is to enable progression and for children to learn. In many different ways, with diverse outcomes, the focus is to enable individualised education for each child. I also share resources to help educators talk to children and families about advocating a neurodiversity-affirming approach. This is usually through texts such as *I Am, You Are: Let's Talk about Disability, Individuality and Empowerment* by Ashley Harris Whaley. This text supports young children to develop an anti-ableist approach and value difference and individuality.

Sarah Thurston (Area SENCO) works frequently with educators to develop personalised planning and strategies. Sarah shares her thoughts on the importance of starting with the child as an individual when planning support:

We begin our journeys as early years educators by learning about child development and typical development pathways or milestones. We learn how to plan appropriate activities to support these developmental milestones. We know how to implement these activities when working with children and appreciate the role of the adult in facilitating learning. We learn to assess children's levels of development and plan for their next steps. These things are our 'bread and butter' practices.

When working with neurodivergent development, we utilise these practices in our Assess, Plan, Do, Review cycles. Rather than using a deficit model of seeking where to implement support, we look to what the child can do currently. Where is their development currently sitting? What does the child need to learn next to support their progress?

Removing the idea of 'age-related expectations' as a pressure that we sometimes feel we have to push to the child towards enables us to value the 'unique child' and utilise a strengths-based, celebratory approach, advocating for diversity.

Making adjustments to suit learning styles by removing barriers and expectations of how play 'should' typically look enables educators to plan provision to promote different ways to learn. A recent example from a setting was following an observation of a child enjoying watching the sand fall to the floor. As Area SENCO, I advised the setting to lower the sand tray to floor level. They had initially seen this as casting; we discussed how this was a possible schema and ways we could support the child's learning through this.

Sarah Thurston (Area SENCO at Doncaster Council)

Thought Provocations

- Do you provide enough opportunities for genuine child-led play?
- Is there an openness/lack of judgement towards all types of self-directed play in your setting or school?

References

Murphy, K. (2023) A Beginner's Guide to Self-Directed Neurodivergent Play. Tapestry. https://tapestry.info/a-beginners-guide-to-self-directed-neurodivergent-play-2.html

Nutbrown, C. (2006) *Key Concepts in Early Childhood Education and Care*. SAGE.

PACEY (2024) Schemas. www.pacey.org.uk/working-in-childcare/spotlight-on/schemas

Piaget, J. (1952) *The Origins of Intelligence in Children*, translated by M. Cook. W.W. Norton & Co.

Child's Name

Play

Neurodivergent children sometimes develop their play in different ways, and it is important to tune in to the individual child's play skills and routines to be able to offer further resources or provocations to increase their engagement and further their learning. Try to observe, wait and listen – are there any schemas or play routines the child is developing? Use the space below to reflect on how the child plays.

Actions

Copyright material from Ann Lowe and Stephen Kilgour (2025), *The Inclusive Early Years Educator*, Routledge

Chapter 8

EXECUTIVE FUNCTION

Executive function refers to a set of cognitive skills that we use to help us plan effectively, focus on an activity, remember key information and juggle multiple tasks. Put simply, it relates to our ability to function throughout the day. Executive function skills are intrinsically linked to self-regulation which we touched on earlier in the book. A child's capacity for learning is enhanced if their executive function skills are working well. This could be in a play scenario or more formal classroom activities later on in their school life. Executive function skills are also vitally important in adult life and help us to navigate our complex existence.

Considering our own executive function skills is a useful starting point for conversations about children's thinking processes.

- How well do we plan?
- How well do we focus?
- How well do we remember key information?
- How well do we juggle multiple tasks?
- How well do we regulate our own emotions?

Everyone will have different reflections when responding to these questions. Some may feel they have particular strengths in certain areas, while finding other aspects challenging. It is important to focus on the impact these individual skills have on our own learning, as well as our productivity and wellbeing.

It is also valuable to evaluate how our executive function skills may be impacted by our circumstances at a given time on a given day. We are all too aware that at certain moments we aren't in the right 'frame of mind' to set about or complete a task. This could be down to being physically unwell, feeling tired or struggling with our mental health. Realistically, a multitude of factors can impact our 'performance'.

Once we are aware of our own challenges associated with this skill set, it can help when reflecting on the difficulties a child may have in these areas, particularly if they are neurodivergent. It is safe to say that a child has a better chance of demonstrating effective executive function skills if they feel safe, secure, calm and content.

DOI: 10.4324/9781003409618-9

Successful application of our executive function skills depends on three broad types of brain function: *working memory*, *mental flexibility* and *self-control*.

Working Memory

Working memory relates to our ability to hold on to information in the short term and use it to impact our reasoning and decision making. An example could be following a simple set of instructions. Our working memory generally has a limited capacity and is different to our ability to memorise facts. It is much more relevant to carrying out activities in the here and now – for example, reading a weight in a recipe and then remembering it for a few moments while you collect the bag of flour and pour it on to the scales.

Our working memory can be affected by various factors, one being distraction. If you are trying to retain a key piece of information, like a house number and street name, but you are being distracted by someone talking to you about something else, then there is an increased chance that you will need to check the information again.

The capacity of a child's working memory will increase over time. A child with learning differences or a disability might struggle to use their working memory as efficiently as their neurotypical peers. This will be amplified if they are finding it difficult to regulate themselves. Consider anyone trying to use their working memory effectively in an environment that is triggering sensory sensitivities or causing distress. Creating an enabling environment for all is key when it comes to providing opportunities for our children to develop their working memory.

Additional support for children in this area could be the use of symbols alongside written words, or the use of Makaton signing when verbally communicating an instruction. When we do this, we 'reinforce' our message by providing more than one cue. A further cue might be modelling expectations as you communicate or using gestures to enhance key words. Resist the temptation to 'normalise' a child's learning and to 'fade' this additional support. There is no need to deliberately make life more difficult for a child with learning differences or a disability.

Mental Flexibility

This is sometimes referred to as 'cognitive flexibility' and relates to our ability to switch our focus between different tasks, adapting and being flexible as we go. Traditionally, we might refer to someone as being a good 'multi-tasker' if they are able to dip in and out of different activities without becoming overwhelmed.

It can also relate to the way that we try new methods of solving a problem if our first strategy isn't working. For some children, it doesn't always come naturally to adapt their thinking 'in the moment', especially if they are becoming frustrated and distressed. We would naturally support any child in this scenario, but it is vital that we are especially sensitive if a child has learning differences that mean tasks that require cognitive flexibility are particularly difficult. Modelling alternative approaches can be a sensible starting point. Reading cues and signs from a child as early as possible is our best chance of avoiding distress. As ever, we should also be continually assessing our environment more generally to ensure that it isn't adding to a child's anxiety.

Children who are finding cognitive flexibility challenging may also become upset when transitioning between one activity and another, or show distress if something happens in their day that they weren't expecting. In both circumstances, providing additional support to these children in preparation for and during these moments is logical. The majority of our attention should be focused on avoidance, rather than planning our response (although this is obviously very important). If we can unpick specific triggers and help a child to have a better understanding of a situation, then we will reduce the chances of distress.

> When someone is in crisis, executive functioning goes offline. It can be near impossible to access 'skills' that require cognitive work. What's needed is self-regulation and co-regulation.
>
> (Price, 2023)

Using symbol support or Makaton signing to reinforce understanding can again be a useful strategy. Visual timetables or 'now and next' boards can aid a child's awareness to support transitions. A simpler approach may be to discuss as a staff team how necessary a transition actually is. We sometimes carry out transitions because they are part of our daily routine, rather than because they are necessary or particularly important. As the majority of early years educators are also aware, transitions can seriously get in the way of high-quality play!

As inclusive educators, we should endeavour to support all of our children when they are finding mental flexibility a challenge.

Self-Control

Self-control is an aspect of 'response inhibition' and refers to a person's ability to regulate emotions and behaviours when faced with impulsive urges or temptations.

Although clearly linked, self-control and self-regulation are not the same thing. Self-control relates specifically to our attempts to repress impulses, whereas self-regulation is linked to our efforts to reduce the frequency and strength of these impulses through the management of our own self-care.

As has been previously mentioned, when working with young children whose self-regulation skills are still developing (as is actually the case with many adults), co-regulation is hugely important in an early years setting or school. Our understanding of child development, particularly in our youngest children, also helps us to have appropriate expectations of how a child may react in a given situation. The part of the brain that is responsible for self-control (the prefrontal cortex) generally isn't fully developed until we are in our mid- to late 20s – which may explain a lot! This part of the brain certainly isn't developed enough by the age of two to enable a toddler to control their urges – so if we are working with under-threes we need to be particularly realistic in our expectations. Considering this type of information should be obvious when planning our environments, but we need to ensure we are being sensitive to a child's current ability to control themself, as opposed to setting them up to fail. This is also very important when considering the children in our group with learning differences.

The consistency of our responses can help a child to develop their self-control skills. We need to reflect on whether our responses might be confusing for a child. If on a given day they are allowed to access a particular resource but on another day they are not, it is understandable that they may become upset. As always, calm, consistent and patient responses from adults are needed if a child is becoming distressed because they are unable to access or use a space or item. Similar to the transition scenario, we must also reflect on our reasons for preventing a child from accessing a space or using a particular resource. Could it be that we are being unnecessarily fussy?

One of the most significant obstacles to a calm and happy environment when working with young children is the issue of taking turns or sharing. We must seek to understand why these moments cause such levels of distress, and our knowledge of child development and understanding of learning differences should help us to respond appropriately in these scenarios. Is it realistic to expect a two- or three-year-old to sit and wait patiently for an extended period while their friend plays with a toy that they are desperate to engage with? Or is it reasonable to presume that a child will have a concept of what five or ten minutes looks or feels like if told to wait for a given period. If we can prevent moments of distress with our consistency, responses and the design of our environment, then everyone wins. It could be as simple as ensuring there are always duplicates of popular items so that conflicts are less likely to arise. Obviously, as children grow, they will naturally encounter opportunities for learning about turn taking and sharing, and we can support these moments sensitively. At all times, we need to make sure we are not setting our children up for failure.

Breaking Down Executive Function Skills Further

In her book *Supporting the Wellbeing of Children with SEND* (2022, pp.142–143), early years specialist Kerry Murphy defines eight executive function skills as follows:

Working Memory – holding information in mind, and being able to retain, recall and act upon that information.

Flexible thinking – tolerating and adapting to change and transition. Unexpected events do not activate too much stress.

Impulse control – being able to think things through before acting and having control over physical and emotional actions.

Emotional control – being able to identify or feel familiar with feelings, to sit with them and keep them in-sync.

Self-direction – being able to monitor and direct oneself independently. Child is motivated, engaged and works towards goals in their play.

Planning and prioritising – being able to engage in play and to sustain attention, make plans and keeping on track.

Task initiation – being able to initiate an activity or play in own way and know how things work.

Organisation – being able to keep track of things physically, emotionally and cognitively.

This added detail helps us to narrow down the aspects of executive function and therefore better identify where a child's strengths lie and where they may need additional support.

Developing a Reflective Approach to Executive Functioning Skills in Doncaster

As an advisory and support team visiting individual children in early years settings in Doncaster, many of our discussions and recommendations cover a range of strategies to develop executive function skills. The case studies detailed below demonstrate examples of strategies that settings in Doncaster are implementing to support children to develop working memory, focus, mental flexibility and self-control.

Reflecting on Working Memory – A Case Study

I visited Hamza at an early years setting in the north of Doncaster. I observed Hamza and spoke to the educators about his learning. Hamza was particularly interested in resources in the mathematical area of the environment. He enjoyed positioning small resources such as bobbins and pebbles around the perimeter of the carpet area and was beginning to develop a particular order and sequence to his patterning. He also showed an interest in counting and alphabet board books making different sounds as he turned the pages. His parents had also observed that Hamza had an interest in jigsaws and puzzles at home, and they described this as the area where he showed the most focus. The team had resourced some puzzles for Hamza, matching his interests to support and develop his learning.

During periods of child-initiated play, Hamza was settled and showed positive responses to his environment. At transition times and periods of adult-led input, Hamza was showing some dysregulated behaviours. Carpet time, tidy-up time, home time and snack time were particularly distressing for Hamza, and he would become upset and frustrated and, on occasion, begin to hurt himself.

We discussed aspects of the day that were necessary for him to access. We agreed that the snack time and home time routine were necessary for Hamza, and that once we had found an approach that helped him, we would move on to supporting him with other points of transition. As Hamza showed an interest in the books and visual images, we agreed on designing a social story around snack time to help Hamza to predict what would happen. We also agreed on Hamza accessing snack alongside a favourite resource (stacking cups) with egg-timer support for two minutes.

We decided on a few short sentences and images to simplify the task and help Hanza to understand the routine (possibly including a visual example). For example:

> At snack time we eat bananas (Hamza's favourite).
> We sit at the table. We can take our favourite toy.
> When the egg timer finishes, we leave the table.

The setting began to share the social story with Hamza for a few days before transitioning to the table, and used objects of reference with the social story to help

Hamza to understand the planned process. After a few weeks of using the social story, the transition to the table was much smoother. But at the same time, the team had noticed that Hamza seemed overwhelmed when joining the table, particularly when there were lots of children. He showed more regulation when there were fewer children at the table. The setting planned to use a specific seat for Hamza at the quietest part of the tables in the classroom where there were fewer children and less noise and movement from adults at snack time. Over the half-term period, Hamza began to make consistently smoother transitions to eat snack at the table.

We agreed on a similar approach at home time to help Hamza with understanding what would happen next. The setting created a social story with images to help him to predict. For example:

> At home time we get our coat and bag from our peg.
> We sit on a chair with our favourite toy.
> Dad picks us up.

By observing Hamza in more detail, the team had also noticed that he showed signs of being overwhelmed at home time. He was particularly distressed when the other children were in the small cloakroom area getting their belongings, and got upset when things became noisy. The setting adapted their routine to enable Hamza to get his belongings before all the other children. They also observed that if children left the setting before Hamza, he would become increasingly upset. The educators adjusted their routine to try to ensure that the door would only be opened when they could see Hamza's parent had arrived, and prioritised him being the first to leave wherever possible.

We reviewed the progress Hamza had made with transitions the following term. We agreed that Hamza's transitions had become smoother and calmer. Hamza was showing increasing regulation and security at the setting. The team felt that consistency was the key to the transitions going well and consistency of strategies had made the biggest difference to Hamza. If something happened to alter this approach, such as a practitioner who wasn't sure how to use the visuals, or a change in the usual routine, or something different going on that day, transitions would become harder. If they stayed consistent to the planned approach, then Hamza was more likely to show increased regulation at previous trigger points. As transitions improved, the practitioners talked about no longer needing the social stories or strategies, but we discussed the benefits of keeping this model for consistency, a sense of safety and security in Hamza's environment. We agreed that the familiarity of using the social story and visual supports could help with developing other routines using the same approach.

Reflecting on Flexible Thinking – A Case Study

Dolly attended a school in the north of Doncaster. She was following a neurodivergent pathway and was referred to the Early Years Inclusion Team. The school was using some additional funding to support Dolly to access a wider range of opportunities in the setting. On my visit to the school, parents and practitioners spoke about how theme days and celebrations were a particularly difficult time for Dolly.

They had observed that when the routine was different to a usual day, Dolly would become dysregulated at school. Her behaviours had become more difficult to manage at home during celebrations, or when they had other family members to visit. We spoke about how the familiar routine at home and school supported Dolly's regulation, and due to this, Dolly was able to access a wider range of learning opportunities and demonstrated higher levels of engagement.

The school had already devised and implemented a visual timetable for Dolly, to enable her to learn more about her environment and the resources on offer for her to access and explore. This had some success, and by presenting Dolly with different, smaller-scale play provisions, supported by a visual timetable, she had shown greater interest in the resources and play opportunities on offer.

Celebrating Eid at school had brought lots of changes to the usual routine, and the school had adapted the visual timetable to support these. Unfortunately, Dolly showed increased signs of dysregulation, and we agreed that the visual timetable wasn't working.

We reflected that maybe some things were always going to be harder for Dolly, even with adaptations, accommodations and help to predict routines – just as teaching in a classroom with fire alarms going off or bricks falling down would be very difficult for us. Everyone has a different level of overwhelm. Dolly needed an increased sense of familiarity brought back into her experience to feel safe within the environment.

We discussed how we could do more to support Dolly during this difficult time by using the visual timetable to *reassure* her about what was going to be familiar in her day, based on her interests, rather than using the visual timetable to *predict* what would happen. For example:

Usual routine	Initial planned visual timetable to aid prediction during celebrations period	Visual timetable to aid regulation and familiarity when celebrating Eid
Welcome time	Welcome time	Welcome time
Water play	Hall time – movement to celebrate Eid	Water play (enhanced with Eid-themed colours)
Painting	Visit from religious figure	Painting (reds, greens, golds)
Playdough	Music concert	Playdough (enhanced with Eid-themed cutters)
Outside	Outside	Outside
Singing	Celebration songs	Singing (familiar nursery rhymes with some Eid celebration songs)

Using the visual timetable to revert to the regular routine helped Dolly to feel a sense of safety and security. Many things going on in and around school were still different and harder to navigate for Dolly, but the familiarity of much of the day helped her to have some periods of regulation during celebrations. Discussions with Dolly's parents about the success of the familiarity aspect of the timetable meant they were encouraged to try similar strategies at home, keeping some of the familiar aspects of Dolly's routine the same to help her regulate and feel safe and secure.

Reflecting on Impulse Control – A Case Study

I visited Rosa at a setting in the south of Doncaster following a referral to the Early Years Inclusion Team for some advice. The early educators at her setting were experiencing challenges in supporting some of Rosa's behaviours – predominantly when accessing continuous provision. Rosa had been accessing the provision for eight weeks, having transitioned from another early years setting with a much smaller room and fewer children. Rosa's current setting could accommodate 60 children, with a large indoor and outdoor environment.

The setting described how Rosa would hit or bite during the session. On occasion Rosa had started to bite herself when redirected away from a situation where she was hurting others. Loud noises were a trigger for Rosa, and she had access to ear defenders. Rosa communicated using predominantly single words, with some two-word phrases.

I worked closely with one of the early years educators to observe Rosa in the indoor environment, focusing on her responses to understand more about her impulsive behaviours. Rosa wore her ear defenders. She approached the large whiteboard area and wanted to do some writing on the board. Two pens were available, and both were being used by other children. Rosa attempted to take a pen from another child who was mark making on the board. The child responded by shouting 'no' and moved the pen away. Rosa responded by hitting the child. An adult supported Rosa to wait for a turn by sitting alongside her nearby the provision. Rosa became increasingly dysregulated when waiting and began kicking her legs and saying 'my turn'. The adult reminded Rosa 'your turn soon'. Rosa's behaviour escalated when waiting. Rosa was reminded 'waiting'. After a short time (approximately 20 seconds), the adult asked another child to let Rosa have a turn, and Rosa accessed the pen and whiteboard.

We discussed possible feelings that may have led to Rosa's behaviours and agreed Rosa had felt a range of emotions during this short period of time:

- Motivation – to access the whiteboard
- Frustration – when she couldn't communicate that she wanted a turn
- Frightened – by the child's response
- Anger – when the pen was not given up and she was unable to access a turn
- Disappointment – leading to further annoyance – when having to wait for a turn
- Fight response – when Rosa felt she could not control the situation
- Enjoyment – when she was able to access the whiteboard

I discussed brain development with the team and how Rosa's instinctive responses happened due the amygdala part of the brain which instigates flight, fight, freeze responses when we feel unsafe or out of control in our environment.

The early years educator commented on how this made sense when thinking of Rosa's behaviours. They had observed that when there were incidents in the environment, Rosa would respond by either hitting out – fight – or running away – flight. Understanding this aspect of neuroscience helped us in planning strategies to build Rosa's feelings of safety, security and control in the environment.

I continued to observe Rosa. She became dysregulated in the domestic play area when more children joined the space. Rosa began to throw things and hit others when the environment was crowded and she couldn't access resources easily. We discussed that any more than four children in an area of the environment was overwhelming for Rosa and a trigger for her fight response.

I observed Rosa at tidy-up time. She seemed unsure of what to do and hid away under a table until the majority of children were sitting on the carpet ready for story time. Rosa then accessed an area of provision before walking nearer to the carpet, but seemed unsure of where to sit. I placed a chair near the carpet area and near to where Rosa was playing. Within a few minutes, Rosa sat down on the chair and listened to the story.

We agreed on the following strategies:

- Use an egg timer e.g. 30 seconds to support Rosa with waiting when she wanted a turn – 'when the timer finishes, it is Rosa's turn'.
- Duplicate resources, if possible, in areas where Rosa shows a preference e.g. pen for whiteboard.
- Limit numbers in areas of provision to provide children with increased access to resources and prevent them from becoming overwhelming and chaotic.
- Place a chair next to the carpet area with a photograph of Rosa on, helping her to find a sense of place at carpet times.
- Use visual prompts to help Rosa know tidy-up time is coming – e.g. first bricks, then tidy up.
- Encouragement to put three items into a box to help Rosa understand the expectation at tidy-up time.
- Use a timer for all children to set the expectation of when tidy-up time will end.
- Build predictable turn taking into the daily routine with Rosa to help her to develop an understanding of taking turns – e.g. posting box with four counters; my turn, your turn, my turn, your turn, finished.
- Use co-regulation techniques in moments of dysregulation.

I discussed many aspects of the strategies and focused on enabling prediction, setting expectation and consistency. These would help Rosa to feel an increased sense of safety and security at the setting, leading to her having increased emotional and impulse control.

Reflecting on a Small-Step Approach to Executive Functioning Skills – A Case Study

I recently accompanied Leanne Webster (Portage Home Visitor) on a visit to a setting in the north of Doncaster. Leanne had worked with Eddie and his family for six months, delivering regular support in the home through the Portage model. Leanne continued to be involved for a period of time as Eddie transitioned into an early years setting. Eddie began to attend a setting for three sessions a week. Mum had shared with Leanne that Eddie was showing some dysregulated behaviours in the setting and that it was becoming increasingly difficult for the educators to manage his behaviours. Mum was worried about Eddie's access to early education.

Leanne and I visited the setting together. The team had been reflective in their approach and shared some of the changes they were trying to help Eddie to settle at nursery. Eddie's key person shared that she had observed Eddie enjoying the leaves outside. She shared that he had engaged in looking at the different leaves and the shapes as they floated down. With this in mind, his key person had dried out some leaves and had them ready at the door for when he was arriving that morning to try to enable a smooth transition by engaging Eddie in something he had shown an interest in. This strategy worked really well, and when Eddie transitioned into the setting, he showed an interest in the different leaves, twisting them between his fingers and looking at the different shapes.

We discussed the challenges that the educators were experiencing and when the crisis points of the day occurred. Eddie's key person shared that it was at transition times mainly, particularly the transition to wash his hands for snack. I observed this part of the session. Eddie was absorbed in looking through some resources with numbers on (numbers are one of his favourite areas of interest). Eddie looked through the numbers and showed a preference for the numbers 4 and 14. Eddie began to sort the number cards into different piles with the 4 and 14 on one side of his body and the other numbers in a pile on the other side. Eddie looked at the educators as we named the numbers. Eddie was in a regulated state and showed complete engagement in looking at the numbers and educator naming them.

After 5–10 minutes, it was tidy-up time, followed by washing hands for snack. Eddie was supported to predict the transition by the staff using an egg timer, visual supports and a song. Eddie pushed the timer and visuals away and continued sorting the numbers. I modelled tidying by placing the numbers in the box, saying, 'numbers in the box'. As soon as I had put them in, Eddie took them back out. His body language and his refusal to put them in the box demonstrated his frustration. Eddie was particularly motivated to continue with the numbers and saw no motivation to begin to put them away for snack.

We talked about the next part of the routine being washing hands and how difficult this transition usually was for Eddie. He would become increasingly dysregulated, often resulting in him hurting others and himself – a fight response. We talked about stripping back the expectations. What did we actually want Eddie to be able to do? We decided on the following outcomes:

- Understand how to put things away
- Develop his self-care skills to wash his hands before eating
- Maintain a regulatory state to be able to access a snack
- Eat something at the setting
- Have longer periods of regulation at the setting

Once we had broken these skills down further, we agreed on some of the adaptations we could make to the provision we were offering:

- We agreed that the number cards were perhaps Eddie's 'comfort blanket' – they made him feel secure in the setting. If these were taken away, so was his feeling of security. We agreed to try to help him to have the numbers nearby at times of transition.
- We agreed to model tidying up alongside him, with other resources not the numbers; today I showed Eddie a box and placed an object inside it – 'Eddie, bricks go in the box' – to help with his understanding of tidying.
- We agreed that taking Eddie to the bathroom area to wash his hands increased his dysregulation and therefore planned to bring a bowl of water to him, to enable him to wash his hands where he was positioned before snack and reduce the need to move areas. This strategy worked well, and following adult modelling, he dipped his hands in the water to wash them.

Eddie had maintained a regulatory state throughout and was able to eat a small portion of a snack he had brought in from home while sitting on the carpet. Using the same strategy over a period of weeks the educators gradually moved the bowl of water nearer to a table, then on to a table. Eddie was then able to sit at a table to wash his hands and eat a preferred snack.

By reverting to what we wanted Eddie to achieve and thinking about other methods to get there, Eddie had achieved the outcomes we had set and developed his self-control and mental flexibility. These strategies had also done wonders for Eddie's key person who felt more capable of developing Eddie's skills, enabling him to learn and make progress.

Thought Provocations

- Are you truly considerate of a child's learning differences when thinking about their executive function skills?

References

Murphy, K. (2022) *Supporting the Wellbeing of Children with SEND: Essential Ideas for Early Years Educators*. London: Routledge. https://doi.org/10.4324/9781003138365

Price, E. (@EmilioLees) (2023, 4 August) Post on X. https://twitter.com/EmilioLees/status/1687381221846683648

Child's Name

Executive Function

Executive function is a set of mental skills that include working memory and flexible thinking. We use these skills every day to learn, work and manage daily life. Difficulties with executive function can make it hard to focus, follow directions and handle emotions, among other things. Neurodivergent children develop executive function skills in different ways, which may be more difficult to interpret. It is important to consider the individual characteristics of the unique child to reflect upon their executive function skills. What behaviours does the individual child exhibit that enables them to plan and achieve goals?

Reflect on:

How does the child remember routines?

How does the child understand the organisation of resources?

Does the child understand where to get a resource in the provision?

Does the child understand how to use self-control?

Actions

Copyright material from Ann Lowe and Stephen Kilgour (2025), *The Inclusive Early Years Educator*, Routledge

Chapter 9

SENSORY REFLECTION

We are taught about our sensory systems from a very young age. It is natural, even when working with babies, to encourage them to use their senses to aid learning. 'Can you smell...?' 'Can you taste...?' 'Can you feel...?' As educators, we are aware of the power of a child's senses to enhance understanding and to reinforce concepts. When we engage multiple senses in an activity, we are generally increasing the likelihood that an experience will be memorable.

If we reflect on our own memories, they are often embellished with sensory elements. This is why memories can be triggered by a follow-up sensory experience. It could be the smell of opening a bottle of suncream reminding you of a happy holiday, the sound of a song that was played at a memorable occasion or the taste of a treat that transports you back to childhood. Whether these sensory reflections trigger feelings of happiness or distress, they are undeniably powerful.

The Eight Sensory Systems
Visual (sight)

The visual system is made up of our eyes which are the 'sensory organs' as well as parts of the central nervous system which together detect and process visible light.

Auditory (hearing)

Auditory input is received through our ears and enables us to gauge a range of information such as whether something is loud or quiet, where a sound is coming from and how far away it is.

Gustatory (taste)

Our taste cells react to food and drink and tell us about flavours, texture and temperature. They are found in our mouths, tongue and throat.

DOI: 10.4324/9781003409618-10

Tactile (touch)

Our tactile system helps us to perceive a wide range of important sensations such as texture, pressure and pain. Touch is also a key aspect of social interaction and relationships.

Olfactory (smell)

Our noses contain sensory receptors which can decipher information about the odours around us. They pass that information along a channel of nerves to the brain. The sense of smell is very powerful, and as well as triggering significant reactions, it can evoke intense memories.

Vestibular (balance)

This is our sense of balance. Information from the vestibular system provides important information about postural orientation. The nerves that control this system are found in the inner ear.

Proprioceptive (movement)

This system tells us where our body parts are in relation to each other, which strengthens our coordination skills. It also informs us how much force to use when we're pushing, pulling, holding or lifting items.

Interoceptive (internal)

This sensory system helps us to understand our body's internal sensations. Examples might be letting us know whether we are feeling hungry or thirsty, or hot/cold.

Reflecting on Sensory Sensitivities and the Learning Environment

The beauty of the human race often lies in our differences. If everyone liked the same foods, the same music or the same art, then life would be pretty dull. When we consider our likes and dislikes, we may not always associate them with our own sensory systems, but the links are actually quite obvious. Think of your favourite food, for instance. Is it spicy or mild? Is it hot or cold? Is it full of flavour or simple and fresh? Our 'tastes', whether linked to the food we consume or otherwise, are unique.

If we consider our ideal learning environment, we are likely to have differences of opinions too. For some, solitary, quiet spaces are most likely to ensure high-quality engagement, whereas others may prefer busy, collaborative opportunities. When we think about our own preferences, it can help us to appreciate the differences in our children's inclination. As with almost every aspect of early education, getting to know our children well is incredibly helpful. We should strive to learn what a child likes, but knowledge about a child's dislikes can be just as powerful. For very young children, or children with learning differences, this may not always be obvious, so we need to make significant efforts to establish this information whenever possible. As well as the child themselves, your relationship with their family will provide you with a good source of information. No one knows them better. Ensure that you have conversations around any sensitivities a child has, or, in even simpler terms, what they dislike – this could be linked to learning environments but, just as importantly, could be around specifics like food and drink. (See Chapter 11 for more around this topic.)

For children with learning differences, and particularly for autistic children, we need to be very aware of aspects of our provision that may unintentionally cause distress. If we become aware of such a detail, then we must act quickly to make adjustments to ensure we are not causing unnecessary harm. We should never take the viewpoint that a child 'just needs to get used to it'. This stance is harmful and wrong. Likewise, to exclude a child from our setting because we are unwilling to make reasonable adjustments is inappropriate and damaging.

Practical Considerations

One of the most common sensitivities for children in a busy nursery setting can be noise. Many people can filter out background noise and remain focused on a task in hand, but for others, this isn't always possible, and these sounds can become distressing. A noisy environment can be unavoidable when large numbers of 3-year-olds are busy with their play, so we must consider ways that can lessen the impact for a child who struggles in this way. If you are lucky enough to have space, then ensuring that quiet zones or rooms are available is a good start, but more likely the use of a support aid such as ear defenders could be helpful. Just as our children's sensory tastes are unique, solutions to sensory sensitivities may well be too – as with any conundrum we face in our learning spaces, we should keep looking for the best solution.

Reflecting on the organisation of our day can be particularly helpful when considering those children with sensory sensitivities. Rigidness of routines can be a contributing factor to distress, especially for autistic children. Chaotic transitions at significant points in the day can be the most challenging for neurodivergent children. For example, a whole-class outside playtime in the middle of the morning at a set time could be the catalyst for distress. We are all aware of the fuss/noise/calamity that can ensue when 30 four-year-olds head to get their coats on at the same time. Moments like these could well be the noisiest and most intimidating point of the day for some of our children. We must be aware if certain moments are especially difficult for our children with learning differences. Most importantly, we must seek to make adjustments to ensure that we can avoid distress where possible. Maybe a child who dislikes this transition because of the busyness and noise could go to get their coat a couple of minutes sooner or carry on with their play until the other children have got their coats on. The same considerations might be made for a child who finds the transition to the dining hall difficult, or who struggles when getting changed for PE. As with almost every aspect of this book, a sound knowledge of each child and their likes and dislikes is very powerful. This information has limited benefit, however, if we don't use it to make adjustments where required. As inclusive educators we should never accept a child's distress as part of their daily routine. Just to reiterate, 'they'll get used to it' is *not* OK.

The Problem with Sensory Rooms

The topic of sensory rooms can be a source of great excitement –- and not just for the children in a setting or school. The prospect of an all-singing, all-dancing space that will magically support our children with learning differences is realistically often wide of the mark. There are also wildly varying standards of sensory room when you visit nurseries and schools. In some circumstances, the room is entirely bare and shabby, used for 1:1 focus tasks, maybe followed by a few bubbles as a reward. In other scenarios, the room is jam-packed with weird and wonderful equipment that provides an environment not too dissimilar to a night club on a Friday evening.

In my experience, there is no such thing as a one-size-fits-all sensory room – a minimalist space can work very effectively if used in a purposeful and appropriate way, and a room packed with the latest technology can also serve a purpose if used appropriately. The biggest problem I observe is that a lot of the time, the educator who is accompanying a child has no understanding of the purpose of their visit to the space. We must ensure that everyone working with a child who visits a sensory room knows the answer to the question 'Why are we doing this?' This is probably the most important self-reflection question anyone working in any stage of education can ask themselves, but for some reason, when it comes to sensory rooms, the response usually goes along the lines of 'a bit of chill-out time' (which can sometimes be OK!).

As with any aspect of our learning environment, sensory rooms should be well planned and based on our observations and knowledge of the children in our care. Their use can fall into two broad categories:

- An extension of our learning environment, where we take advantage of engaging and motivating technology/resources to reinforce understanding of, for example, cause and effect.
- An area for children with sensory sensitivities to regulate with the support of a familiar adult.

Making this important distinction should be our first step when establishing our 'why?' In an ideal world, the space would be able to accommodate both aspects. Once we are aware of the broad rationale for the sensory room, we then need to plan the space so that it will serve a purpose. Contrary to popular belief, equipment for a sensory room doesn't have to be hi-tech or expensive – although there are plenty of amazing machines available that can enhance these spaces. As with any aspect of our learning environment, a sensory room should be responsive to the needs of the children in a particular group, so from one year to the next, a room may be used in different ways.

It is especially important if we are using a sensory room as a calming space that we consider what will be helpful for the individual children who will spend time there. Receiving input from a child's family, as well as any specialists or therapists who are involved, would be sensible. We also need to establish whether this room is part of our 'preventative' or 'response' plans – is this going to be part of a child's daily routine or just used when they are experiencing a level of distress? It might be that it is both.

Over- and Under-Stimulation

You may have heard the term 'stim' or 'stimming' when working with an autistic child. Stim is a shortened word for 'self-stimulation', and autistic children may stim for a variety of reasons. Stimming may involve movements, use of objects or sometimes vocal sounds. Importantly, it doesn't always mean that something is 'wrong' or that a child is distressed.

One scenario might be that a child is trying to self-regulate their emotions, and their stimming is helping them to do this. Another situation that we should be aware of is if a child is stimming because they are experiencing too much or too little sensory input. For example, a child may stim during particularly busy and noisy times of the day at nursery or school (they are 'over-stimulated'). This would give an indication that adjustments might be necessary to support the child. Conversely, a child may stim because they are experiencing under-stimulation. In this situation, it might be helpful to offer opportunities for additional sensory input. Many children enjoy deep pressure at times like these, like big hugs or firm massages. Always be led by the child and seek advice from an occupational therapist if you are unsure of what is appropriate in terms of equipment or techniques. Rather than waiting for a child to become distressed before providing additional sensory input, it makes sense to build regular sensory opportunities across a child's day if these activities help a child to feel regulated. A routine of this sort is sometimes referred to as a 'sensory diet'. Some children's sensory diet might consist of lots of big physical activities like bouncing on a trampoline or rolling big tyres, whereas others might get more benefit from a calm and quiet hand massage to start the day. As an inclusive educator, we should strive to learn what supports a child's wellbeing, and therefore enhances their potential for learning.

Educator's View – Fifi Benham (Deputy Manager, Early Years Educator and SENCO)

Early years settings are typically loud, busy and bright. While a lively atmosphere isn't a negative thing, there are many reasons this may be inaccessible.

Having dedicated sensory rooms is wonderful, but it is not realistic for a lot of settings in terms of cost and space available. However, there are still ways to create quieter spaces within the setting. Building forts, using tents or even just dividers to break up the space. In my own practice, we repurposed a bed tent someone had outgrown to create a cosy space that blocked out some of the overhead lighting.

Sensory toys give people a way to regulate their nervous system through providing predictable, repetitive sensory input. The types of sensations or movements children seek will vary and so it's important to consider if your sensory toys are providing a range of different sounds, sights and tactile sensations. This is also a good starting point for settling, especially for neurodivergent children. Asking during admissions what the child likes to look at, touch or listen to in addition to the usual questions about favourite toys can give valuable insight into how best to make them feel safe.

In trying to make the whole of your space as accessible as possible, it's important to observe if particular children avoid certain areas and examine why. We know that neurodivergent children often either constantly seek out or very much avoid 'messy play'. Sometimes investigating the specific reason for avoidance means we can open up the area for a child. In my own practice, I've come across children whose dislike of messy play came from not liking any residue on their hands or not liking having to wash their hands after, and several children who were only actually avoiding wearing an apron!

The environment can also be very overwhelming for staff. As an autistic practitioner, feeling over-stimulated at work is definitely something I've experienced. An understanding that your team have their own needs and preferences is essential, as well as creating opportunities for staff to feel safe voicing these things. Steps such as flexibility in rotas, ability to take breaks, taking groups of children out for focus activities, leading story times or running a sensory activity are some of the many ways staff can be given time to regulate while still actively supporting children.

Developing a Reflective Approach to Sensory Processing in Doncaster
Reflecting on Personalised Learning Plans

Using 'All About Me' plans to support each individual child's learning has helped to raise the importance of knowing and planning for a child's sensory sensitivities in Doncaster. Writing these in collaboration with the child's family improves partnership working with parents and carers. Sharing knowledge and observations about their child can greatly increase the chances of a child feeling safer, more secure and settled as they transition into an early years setting.

Unfortunately, in our line of work, we will sometimes encounter families who have taken their children to a number of early years providers until they find the 'right fit'. When talking to parents about their reasons for changing settings, they often refer to the learning environment being 'too busy', 'too noisy' or just 'too much' for their child.

When considering an early years provider, we are always keen to encourage parents to visit a range of settings – childminders, nurseries, school nurseries – to 'get a feel' for how their child may find the setting. From the very moment parents enter an early years setting, how they feel and how they experience the sights/sounds will likely be one of the deciding factors in whether they place their child at a setting or not.

Supporting children by planning for their unique sensory processing, before they start, can be really helpful for settings in increasing a child's regulation and positive experiences.

Sensory Sensitivities – The Learning Environment Case Study

Sonny attended a setting in the north of Doncaster. Sonny had been identified as neurodivergent and had involvement from health professionals when he was referred to the Early Years Inclusion Team by the setting. The nursery requested some support and guidance to help engage Sonny in his learning. They had found that, at times during the session, staff were finding it difficult to engage Sonny in aspects of the routine. The visual supports that were already in place were not working to help him at moments such as carpet time or group time.

I visited Sonny at the nursery and began by observing him in the indoor environment. The environment was fantastically resourced with many opportunities for children to take learning in a range of directions, but it was a small room with 18–20 children accessing the 2–5s room and a further 10–15 on the other side of a gated area accessing the 0–2 room. It was a hive of activity, a laboratory of possibilities, but it was also very busy and noisy inside.

At snack time, Sonny found it difficult to stay seated for a short period of time and benefitted from an egg-timer support to sit and eat for a few minutes to finish his snack. Once finished, while his peers were continuing to eat or accessing continuous provision, Sonny moved around the environment, walking from side to side in between furniture, retracing the same pathway. At times, he would move his hands across the top of shelves and cupboards, removing anything on top of them and sliding resources to the floor. The educators attempted to use visual supports and redirected to different resources, but he seemed to find it difficult to identify with the visuals he was shown. On first impressions, Sonny presented as a little one who was feeling overwhelmed by the noise and the busyness, and was stimming to make it through the time that he was enduring the indoor environment.

After a short time in the indoor environment, Sonny accessed the outdoor environment and responded very differently. Sonny approached an adult to instigate a game of throwing and catching a ball. This evolved into a rolling and ball-following game developed by Sonny. He accessed the digging area using a spade and bucket, and enjoyed moving himself up and down a large wooden train, pretending to drive. There was little stimming observed and he showed increased access and engagement with the learning opportunities on offer. The outdoors offered him more space and less noise, and he became more regulated (in short – much happier).

We discussed Sonny's possible sensory sensitivities based on what we had observed, and the educators shared that Sonny's family had also observed that in busy, noisy spaces Sonny was more likely to show signs of dysregulation.

The nursery had also developed a sensory room onsite, which we visited with Sonny. Sonny transitioned well to the sensory room with verbal prompts and seemed encouraged to explore the environment. In the sensory room, the nursery manager and I observed that Sonny showed increased instances of verbal communication, making repeated sound patterns, and sought out the adult to ask them to make a toy function or repeat an action. Sonny showed particular interest in a spinning top, verbally and physically prompting the adult to make the top spin again. This was the most verbal communication we had observed throughout the visit. We discussed the levels of wellbeing and engagement we had noticed. We surmised from our discussions that Sonny's levels of wellbeing and engagement were much higher in the outdoor area and sensory room. As a result, we began to put a plan together to increase the time Sonny accessed the outdoors and the sensory room to enable him to learn and develop in an environment that suited his sensory sensitivities.

The nursery manager asked me to lead a staff meeting to share more about the adjustments we had planned for Sonny. I was thrilled with the inclusive approach the educators showed in being on board with personalised planning for Sonny. As I started discussing Sonny's sensory experience of the world, many of the educators started to shift their thinking. Comments such as 'I'd never thought about it like that' and 'wow, yes I get it now' meant that they were very much on board with the way we could think about provision and routine in a child centred way for Sonny.

Reflecting on Personalised Sensory Planning – A Case Study

Jay attended a setting in the north of Doncaster and had been referred to the Early Years Inclusion Team by the nursery due to differences in his development and learning. They had observed that Jay preferred to lie across the carpet areas on his tummy or his back for much of the session, sometimes moving his body up and down. When Jay was sitting up, he preferred to have a practitioner behind him to lean on and seemed to be more able to access learning when he was positioned in this way. The educators had also observed that Jay would sometimes present as 'floppy' when he moved around the provision, preferring to crawl or roll to items that he wanted to access. The staff were also finding it difficult to increase Jay's motivation to access learning activities and had observed that he seemed under-stimulated at times.

I visited Jay at the setting and spent time with his key person, learning about Jay and discussing aspects of his development. Jay was accessing a stickle bricks activity when I arrived at the setting, and he enjoyed sticking the bricks together to make a model. Jay's key person supported his body from the back as he built. She commented that wherever she sat, Jay would move to place his body to lean his back on her. The educator described how he had made the exact same model each day and enjoyed repeating the experience. Jay had a strength in visual memory and was able to represent the same model on consecutive days, without a visual prompt or photograph. Jay's key person commented that he showed lots of motivation while completing this activity, but afterwards it was hard to stimulate Jay to be involved in any other aspect of learning. They observed that his levels of involvement had reduced and they were finding it difficult to increase them.

After 10–15 minutes of observing Jay building with the stickle bricks he placed the model in front of him on the carpet area. He then rolled on to his front and then on to his back, holding the model above in his hands turning it over and looking at it. Jay made sounds as he played with the model.

After a few minutes, Jay's key person initiated a tickle game with Jay, moving his hand down his arm. Jay responded with a wide smile and giggle and moved the practitioner's hand to repeat the action. Jay responded each time with a giggle, and Jay's key person continued the interaction. After a few minutes, Jay rolled over and remained lying on the carpet for several minutes. Jay's key person attempted to show Jay different objects to engage him in other activities, but he seemed distant and discarded the items.

Later in the session, when Jay sat up from lying down, his key person asked him if he wanted to access outside, and Jay followed his key person's lead and pointed to the climbing equipment. Jay moved across the climbing frame and positioned his body with the top half always slightly further forward than the bottom half. Jay moved across the equipment, holding on and looking carefully at each step. Jay's key person demonstrated some early response games (e.g. peek-a-boo), and Jay responded with big smiles and giggles. Jay pointed to the bike area and accessed a tricycle. Jay found it difficult to use his strength to move the wheels but enjoyed being pulled and pushed to move on the wheeled vehicle.

We discussed strategies to support Jay's next steps and agreed:

- A referral to occupational therapy would be helpful to gain specialist advice on ways to support Jay's proprioception and develop his core strength.
- To offer Jay a bean bag or similar cushion to enable Jay to have the feeling of body support (i.e. the feeling of leaning on an adult).
- To offer Jay a range of resources to support his proprioception (i.e. exercise balls, peanut balls, soft play cylinders for him to roll and position himself on).
- To plan extended opportunities in the outside area to support Jay in further developing his physical skills and core strength and increase his confidence at positioning his body.
- To use increased Intensive Interaction techniques to enhance Jay's levels of involvement and stimulate his wellbeing and increase his arousal levels to enable increased access to learning activities.

Reflecting on Professional Development to Learn More about Sensory Processing in Doncaster

My colleague Shelley Petta (Early Years Inclusion Officer and Lead for Assessment) established a 0–60 months Moderation Network several years ago in Doncaster. The group is made up of a small number of early educators who have a passion for connecting with others to share good practice and to celebrate children's progress and attainment in the early years. The group plan and facilitate networking opportunities for early years educators and represent a range of education backgrounds, including owners and managers of private settings, mainstream teachers and teachers in specialist provision. This range of experience enables us to learn from each other and cover a range of CPD topics through moderation sessions.

I met Jo Worrall (Early Years Lead at Coppice School) and Danielle Scott (Early Years Lead at North Ridge School) through the moderation group. Both Jo and Danielle are teachers working in specialist schools in Doncaster. They have a wealth of knowledge about sensory differences and sensitivities, and a deep understanding of how to use each child's unique sensory profile in their setting to plan their provision and routine. Early educators have greatly benefitted from a range of advice and support from

Jo and Danielle in the moderation sessions; discussing children's learning profiles together has supported planning for next steps.

At a recent moderation session, Jo and Danielle were able to share information about proprioception and how to identify proprioception differences through observations of a child: possibly seeking pressure, stamping, rocking or enclosing themselves. Jo and Danielle shared practical advice about ways to support this through the use of equipment such as sensory socks, fit balls, peanut balls, brushes and resistance bands. This prompted much conversation about the importance of considering sensory aspects when planning provision for a child.

Jo shares their views on the importance of sensory reflection below:

One of the most vital tools in your practitioner's tool kit is observation. This is probably more important with pupils who have SEND or our non-speaking pupils. Every behaviour or action we observe should be reflected on: Is this communication? If only we take the time to tune in and 'listen', much can be discovered about an individual child. To the unobservant, these behaviours can easily be missed or misconstrued, which is why it is so vital to step back, despite the hustle and bustle of a busy environment, take a breath and watch.

There are many questions to ask yourself when observing, but it is always a good starting point to think of Maslow's hierarchy of need. Are their basic needs being met? Is this what the behaviour is telling us? Have they had a drink? Are they hungry? Are they uncomfortable? Are they seeking a connection?

If all of these have been met, we can move on to the next set of questions. This is where it is also vital to know the child, know them holistically and know them through their parents and carers, working in collaboration to better understand and interpret what you are seeing.

Are the behaviours happening in certain areas/environments or at certain times of the day? Could the behaviour be indicating hunger? Do they need to go to the toilet/bowel movement/urinate at similar times of the day? The muddled feelings surrounding this may indicate difficulties in interoception.

Is it in response to transitioning from one place to another? Does the type of flooring affect how they move or behave? Is the flooring patterned? Does the flooring change from one texture to another? These could indicate visual overstimulation or gravitational insecurities.

Do they stamp or are they heavy-footed when walking? Do they throw objects, enjoy or give tight hugs and squeezes, jump or tap objects? These could relate to the child seeking proprioceptive input. As practitioners, there are many ways in which we can support this in all learning environments including therapy balls, Thera bands, trampettes and a positive touch policy, so massage and movement therapies such as TACPAC and Story Massage can take place, all with the consent of both parent and child.

Lingering on or refusal of certain textures, media or experiences could relate to the need to seek tactile experiences or a child who is tactile defensive and doesn't like or becomes overwhelmed by certain sensory experiences. Making reasonable adjustments in practice helps to ensure the child is included. For example, for a child who doesn't enjoy finger painting or paint exploration, the use of a ziplock bag with paint sealed inside means they can still achieve and explore without the need for directly touching the paint.

A child who likes to hang upside down, spin or enjoys movements could indicate the need to seek out vestibular stimulation.

It is also important to mention stimming. Stimming, or self-stimulatory behaviour, should never be stopped. Watching and knowing the child well can help to identify stimming and recognise that this is an important part of their self-regulation.

There are numerous reasons a child will behaviour a certain way, and it is down to the practitioners who know child best to try to interpret them and, with the support of specialist setting outreach, SEND advisory educator or sensory occupational therapy support, put strategies in place.

It is also vital to consider how the child is developing and what steps could be next. Tapestry's SEND descriptors based on Development Matters 2012 adds much more detail to the earliest stages in development and have contributed towards our developmental Progression Maps at Coppice.

In finding more about how a child is developing and at what stage, resources and expectations can be more aligned and will help to set and achieve outcomes. It is also important to start to unpick the differences in schematic play, which may be developmentally linked and repetitive play, which is not a hindrance in development. Repetitive play in autistic children is vital in helping them to make sense of the world; repetition provides the understanding of sameness, and sameness supports them to be regulated. If the world is more predictable, it's a less confusing place to be, which is why repetition is often seen.

Their developmental stage may also explain why some children mouth toys or resources, but this could equally be pica.

Reflection and learning about how a child experiences the world through their senses, and adjusting practice, is vital to enable access to learning and education.

Jo Worrall (Early Years Lead at Coppice School)

Sensory reflection continued to be an interest in Doncaster. I became aware of Sadie Charlton (Sensory Occupational Therapist) through my colleague Abi Kershaw (Area SENCO). Abi and Sadie met while both attending training on Trauma Informed Approaches and shared a mutual interest in developing practice in relation to sensory-friendly education spaces.

At that point, Sadie was beginning to develop Sensory Pie – a resource for early years and primary schools to aid the creation of optimal learning environments for every child, founded on the promotion of sensory-friendly practice.

Aiming to put sensory reflection firmly on the agenda in Doncaster, we invited Sadie to deliver an input at a recent Early Years SENCO Cluster event. Educators who attended the event commented on the possible future impact on their practice around sensory considerations for individual children. As Sadie spoke about each of the senses in turn, educators commented how they identified children in each of their settings who they thought showed sensitivities to some of these. Identifying these helped in planning provision for an individual child.

Thought Provocations

- Are practical adjustments made in your setting/school to ensure that children's sensory sensitivities are genuinely considered?
- Is there an understanding as to 'why' a child might be responding in a certain way? Are they over- or under-stimulated?

Child's Name

Sensory Reflection

Each individual is unique in their sensory profile. It is important to understand a child's unique profile to discover the types of resources or activities that will best captivate them. Appropriate sensory stimulation can increase children's concentration and focus, and find a calm enabling state for them to learn and develop. Many children with learning differences benefit from being in an environment where they are neither over- nor under-stimulated. Reflecting on a child's sensory sensitivities can help with planning appropriate sensory-soothing play and adapting provision to meet individual children's needs. Reflect upon children's sensitivities and responsiveness in the various areas and add actions where appropriate.

Visual (sight)

Actions

Copyright material from Ann Lowe and Stephen Kilgour (2025), *The Inclusive Early Years Educator*, Routledge

Child's Name

Sensory Reflection

Each individual is unique in their sensory profile. It is important to understand a child's unique profile to discover the types of resources or activities that will best captivate them. Appropriate sensory stimulation can increase children's concentration and focus, and find a calm enabling state for them to learn and develop. Many children with learning differences benefit from being in an environment where they are neither over- nor under-stimulated. Reflecting on a child's sensory sensitivities can help with planning appropriate sensory-soothing play and adapting provision to meet individual children's needs. Reflect upon children's sensitivities and responsiveness in the various areas and add actions where appropriate.

Auditory (hearing)

Actions

Copyright material from Ann Lowe and Stephen Kilgour (2025), *The Inclusive Early Years Educator*, Routledge

Child's Name

Sensory Reflection

Each individual is unique in their sensory profile. It is important to understand a child's unique profile to discover the types of resources or activities that will best captivate them. Appropriate sensory stimulation can increase children's concentration and focus, and find a calm enabling state for them to learn and develop. Many children with learning differences benefit from being in an environment where they are neither over- nor under-stimulated. Reflecting on a child's sensory sensitivities can help with planning appropriate sensory-soothing play and adapting provision to meet individual children's needs. Reflect upon children's sensitivities and responsiveness in the various areas and add actions where appropriate.

Gustatory (taste)

Actions

Copyright material from Ann Lowe and Stephen Kilgour (2025), *The Inclusive Early Years Educator*, Routledge

Child's Name

Sensory Reflection

Each individual is unique in their sensory profile. It is important to understand a child's unique profile to discover the types of resources or activities that will best captivate them. Appropriate sensory stimulation can increase children's concentration and focus, and find a calm enabling state for them to learn and develop. Many children with learning differences benefit from being in an environment where they are neither over- nor under-stimulated. Reflecting on a child's sensory sensitivities can help with planning appropriate sensory-soothing play and adapting provision to meet individual children's needs. Reflect upon children's sensitivities and responsiveness in the various areas and add actions where appropriate.

Tactile (touch)

Actions

Copyright material from Ann Lowe and Stephen Kilgour (2025), *The Inclusive Early Years Educator*, Routledge

Child's Name

Sensory Reflection

Each individual is unique in their sensory profile. It is important to understand a child's unique profile to discover the types of resources or activities that will best captivate them. Appropriate sensory stimulation can increase children's concentration and focus, and find a calm enabling state for them to learn and develop. Many children with learning differences benefit from being in an environment where they are neither over- nor under-stimulated. Reflecting on a child's sensory sensitivities can help with planning appropriate sensory-soothing play and adapting provision to meet individual children's needs. Reflect upon children's sensitivities and responsiveness in the various areas and add actions where appropriate.

Olfactory (smell)

Actions

Copyright material from Ann Lowe and Stephen Kilgour (2025), *The Inclusive Early Years Educator*, Routledge

Child's Name

Sensory Reflection

Each individual is unique in their sensory profile. It is important to understand a child's unique profile to discover the types of resources or activities that will best captivate them. Appropriate sensory stimulation can increase children's concentration and focus, and find a calm enabling state for them to learn and develop. Many children with learning differences benefit from being in an environment where they are neither over- nor under-stimulated. Reflecting on a child's sensory sensitivities can help with planning appropriate sensory-soothing play and adapting provision to meet individual children's needs. Reflect upon children's sensitivities and responsiveness in the various areas and add actions where appropriate.

Vestibular (balance)

Actions

Copyright material from Ann Lowe and Stephen Kilgour (2025), *The Inclusive Early Years Educator*, Routledge

Child's Name

Sensory Reflection

Each individual is unique in their sensory profile. It is important to understand a child's unique profile to discover the types of resources or activities that will best captivate them. Appropriate sensory stimulation can increase children's concentration and focus, and find a calm enabling state for them to learn and develop. Many children with learning differences benefit from being in an environment where they are neither over- nor under-stimulated. Reflecting on a child's sensory sensitivities can help with planning appropriate sensory-soothing play and adapting provision to meet individual children's needs. Reflect upon children's sensitivities and responsiveness in the various areas and add actions where appropriate.

Proprioceptive (movement)

Actions

Copyright material from Ann Lowe and Stephen Kilgour (2025), *The Inclusive Early Years Educator*, Routledge

Child's Name

Sensory Reflection

Each individual is unique in their sensory profile. It is important to understand a child's unique profile to discover the types of resources or activities that will best captivate them. Appropriate sensory stimulation can increase children's concentration and focus, and find a calm enabling state for them to learn and develop. Many children with learning differences benefit from being in an environment where they are neither over- nor under-stimulated. Reflecting on a child's sensory sensitivities can help with planning appropriate sensory-soothing play and adapting provision to meet individual children's needs. Reflect upon children's sensitivities and responsiveness in the various areas and add actions where appropriate.

Interoceptive (internal)

Actions

Copyright material from Ann Lowe and Stephen Kilgour (2025), *The Inclusive Early Years Educator*, Routledge

Chapter 10

CHILD'S VOICE

Much of our work in early childhood education rightly focuses on what we observe in our learning environment. What are children engaging with and in which areas are they showing most 'involvement'? What do they appear to like and what are they not so keen on? In some ways, we are interpreting a child's actions and making judgements about what they would say about their learning if they could communicate it effectively. Are we, however, placing enough emphasis on actual conversations/communications about learning with our children?

Metacognition

Metacognition sounds quite a grand term, but it basically refers to the way that we think about and reflect on our own learning. This might initially seem like a daunting task with a three- or four-year old, but some common practices in the early years very much lend themselves to providing these opportunities.

Many settings choose to create 'learning journals' which tell the story of a child's learning. These can take many forms, from individual scrapbook-style paper journals to more modern online systems. The reforms in the EYFS have encouraged us to spend less time making assessments for assessment's sake, but this has led in some circumstances to us throwing the baby out with the bathwater. It is not a good use of educator time to seek photographic or video evidence for every aspect of learning over the course of a year for every child in a group. However, that should not mean we disregard the positives that come from recording and sharing certain moments with children, families and colleagues. As with anything in education, we should strive for a balance, particularly where workload is concerned.

If a setting has chosen to make paper journals, it is important to remind ourselves who and what they are for. In some circumstances, so much effort is made by practitioners to produce beautifully presented journals as keepsakes for families, and therefore these often sit high up on shelves in a setting, well out of reach of the children who feature in them, in case they get spoiled. This is such a shame,

DOI: 10.4324/9781003409618-11

especially when there is an opportunity to engage children in discussions about their learning.

Another style of recording that has gained popularity is a 'floorbook'. This also tends to have a scrapbook style, but there is one large book for a whole group or class rather than individual records. The intention is that this book is very much shareable on a day-to-day basis with children in a group. A key aspect is that the floorbook should contain children's thoughts and ideas as well as any media that may be inserted.

One of the most powerful features of using digital technology to create online journals is the ability to record and share videos of the children in play. If a picture paints a thousand words, then a video must surpass that figure significantly.

A one-minute video of learning can:

- Provide educators with a greater understanding of what a child knows and can do, enabling them to better consider what the child's next steps might be.
- Enable families to have an insight into how their child engages and interacts away from the home environment (as a parent who has received updates of this type, they can be so fascinating!).
- Prompt discussions with children about learning and achievements, allowing a child to *find their voice*.
- Create opportunities for reflection about the quality of provision – often this can centre around the interactions (or interruptions) we make as adults. Seeing yourself at work can help you to fine-tune your own approach, as well as facilitate the sharing of high-quality teaching with colleagues. It can also feel like a celebration when reviewing footage as a team, highlighting strengths as well as possible adjustments that can be made.

It is rare that you will meet a child who doesn't enjoy watching videos of themselves. While researching digital documentation in early childhood education, Kate Cowan and Rosie Flewitt found the following:

> Viewing video of themselves and their peers appeared to be particularly engaging for the children, which suggests that the capacity to include moving image and sound in digital documentation presents new possibilities for capturing and sharing moments of learning in ways that are especially meaningful to young children.
>
> (Cowan and Flewitt, 2021, p.16)

Focusing on metacognition as an educator can help children to develop a deeper understanding of themselves as a learner. Moving forward, it helps them to understand tasks more clearly, while considering approaches and strategies effectively.

Valuing a Child's Voice

Aside from the benefits to a child's future metacognitive skills, communication between an educator and a child gives the child an *active voice*. It is important that we listen to what we are being told, and use this information to support our teaching. It is yet another instrument in our 'observational toolkit', which can help us to shape our provision.

For children with learning differences or disabilities, it isn't always as straightforward to ascertain their thoughts on a particular moment of learning. It is crucial, however, that we place value in trying to find out what every child is thinking. As is so often the case when working with children, we have the best chance of doing this if we know them extremely well, and a trusting bond has been established. This doesn't necessarily happen quickly, and we must invest time in establishing these high-quality relationships.

The term 'child's (or pupil's) voice' in education has become synonymous with children who may need extra support. This is because when creating documents like Education, Health and Care Plans, we are encouraged to include a child's views on what is important to them. This is a welcome addition to the process of seeking additional assistance in a setting or school, though it is only valuable if appropriate emphasis is placed on the concept. As many children who are the subject of EHC plans have communication differences, the likelihood is that they will need a form of extra support in order to contribute their thoughts.

As mentioned earlier, regular opportunities for children to observe their own learning can be helpful, with a close educator able to interpret responses for children with complex support needs. Children who have an understanding of symbol representation may be able to tell you about their preferences using a 'chat board' or communication book. Lo-tech or hi-tech eye-gaze systems could also be used to ascertain a child's favourite activity or area of the environment.

It is always helpful to engage families in discussions around a child's preferences, as the vast majority of the time they know their own child best – regardless of whether a nursery or school might suggest differently. See Chapter 11.

Educator's View – Emma Pinnock
(Teacher, trainer and advocate)

For many of us who have been in education for a while, the idea of 'pupil voice' has been promoted and enhanced through many initiatives, but sometimes the importance of 'voice' can become diluted by the focus on outcomes and data.

So why is 'voice' important? And why, specifically, is a child's voice important to recognise and develop?

Culturally, we are now less inclined to say that 'a child should be seen and not heard'. As we have become more aware of wellbeing and the importance of safeguarding, we have recognised the wider reasons for a child's voice to be heard, ensuring that 'pupil voice' is on the agenda. Although these are very important reasons to highlight a 'child's voice', there are more subtle reasons to enhance and recognise their contribution.

My inner voice

A child's 'inner voice' is rich and imaginative; it simultaneously creates fantasy and reality. Happiness and sadness. Risk and safety. Dreams and aspirations. All of which leads to their personality development, their consciousness, their values systems and more. Openly embracing a child's voice gives educators insights into and opportunities to learn from this inner voice.

Our voice shapes how we learn, but to be heard helps us to connect

Hearing a child's voice is not only informative, but also formative. As human beings, we – to varying degrees – value connection and belonging. We are best connected when we feel listened to and heard. Hearing a child's voice without the need to change its direction will be most beneficial to that child's wellbeing and understanding of self. Our voice is the way we connect with our world. Our tone changes to share emotion, our words shape our reality and desire for security, our voice is the power we hold. Allowing children to engage with their autonomy by using their voice, allows them to understand their personal influence on their world and as we are responsible for educating the world's future leaders, we have to responsibly teach them the power of their voice.

What if my voice differs, what if my way of communicating is different?

This wouldn't be a contribution by me if I didn't discuss voices that are distinctive, be that through experience, biology or simply the colourful tapestry of life. As educators, we can all recall the child whose communication style differs to ours, the pre-verbal child, the child who communicates through actions, the child who has not yet developed their inner voice, or the child who, due to life experiences, continues to use tears/behaviour to communicate.

This version of 'voice' is a true challenge for education, and as inclusion evolves, this continues to be a challenge that requires our attention, because the voice of every child, regardless of what we hear, colours our understanding and approach.

Creating a bridge of understanding is the only way to communicate when the language we hear is not the language we speak. The bridge of understanding can be communicated through body language, visuals, sign or simply the tone in which we share our thoughts. The initial construction of this bridge can only really be in the hands of the adult whose voice is trying to reach those who 'voice' distinctively. The bridge construction can only really be completed when the distinctive child's voice is heard, and they are given the tools to construct their understanding and approach to communicating with their world.

Developing a Reflective Approach to Advocating for the Child's View in Doncaster

In Doncaster, over the last few years we have been considering more ways to develop the child's voice and families' voices as the golden thread that runs through all aspects of personalised planning for children with SEND. I was recently invited to an event in Doncaster, entitled Achieving a Shared Understanding of Co-production through the Four Cornerstones, where young people with SEND spoke passionately about their views, their experiences (positive and negative) and the importance of educators understanding how children were feeling about their experience of education to be able to develop true engagement.

One student at the event spoke powerfully of how overwhelmed he would sometimes become in education establishments and the impact of this on how he would think and feel about educators and school. This resulted in a standing ovation and many educators commenting on their reflections on his lived experience of schooling and the changes that need to be made. A priority for Doncaster Early Years Inclusion Team is to use the voices of lived experience to shape policy and practice in relation to SEND.

In early years, we strive to be continually reflective in our practice and documentation to entrench the voice of the child and use this voice to influence, change and adapt practice with our authority. Mandy Haddock, (Early Years Inclusion Officer; Lead for SEND) has transformed the process of early identification, a significant influence in this change has been within her role as a manager within a specialised provision.

Mandy describes the changes:

> Working directly with children, families, practitioners, students and external agencies enables me to have a clear understanding of barriers, challenges and identifying the gaps with SEND.
>
> With this understanding, I have created and changed documentation and approaches to SEND. This has been over a relatively short period of time. The impact of these changes ensures a greater focus on the voice of each individual child, particularly in relation to the Early Years Inclusion Team, who can now deliver a block of intense support or funding without the need for the child to have a diagnosis.
>
> Providers are required to have regard to and document individual needs and interests of children through their eyes. The referral asks providers to detail information based on the child's perspective. This includes videos, photographs and an 'All About Me' page. The questions within the request and documentation are strengths based and terminology is fundamental. There has been a shift in culture and attitudes where providers no longer feel they need to focus on the child's differences to access more funding.
>
> Mandy Haddock, (Early Years Inclusion Officer; Lead for SEND)

Another way we have moved towards upholding children's views in their assessments is through improving the information collated as part of the two-year check. Shelley Petta, Early Years Inclusion Officer leading on the two-year check has rigorously reviewed the documentation and there is now the facility to add video clips to the two-year check documentation to capture the child's individualism in more ways than a written description could:

During the Covid pandemic, Doncaster's Community Nursery Nurses, who carry out the two-year health review, were reporting that parents were enthusiastically sharing videos and photos of their children engaged in a range of activities. The Integrated Progress Check steering group felt this would strengthen parental confidence and understanding around how their view of their child would be central to the Integrated Progress Check. We looked at ways clips can be shared within the document itself.

The child's voice and parent's voice were crucial, and we wanted to remove as many barriers as possible, so we encouraged parents to attach voice notes and jottings in their home language which could then be reflected upon in the face-to-face meeting with the nursery and, if required, the community nursery nurse. It was vital that a holistic picture of the child was gathered as we were becoming increasingly aware that Covid had impacted significantly on the way children presented in settings compared with in the security of their own homes. These changes placed value on the child's voice and parent's voice as advocators for their own learning.

Shelley Petta (Early Years Inclusion Officer
– Lead for Integrated Progress Check)

My colleague Suzanne Walton (Early Years Inclusion Officer Leading on Schools) has also developed further understanding of the benefits of floorbooks in supporting children's voices to be upheld and influential in schools. Examples of floorbooks being used effectively really demonstrate visually the learning journey children have taken to achieve next steps and are effective as a celebratory document.

Willow Primary School in Doncaster describe the benefits of using floorbooks below:

In Reception, the use of floorbooks became central to our daily practice as we implemented the new framework. They are active, collaborative documents that we use to celebrate, record and review our curriculum across the seven areas of learning. With language, communication and vocabulary at the heart, we gain insight into the impact of learning and experiences for all children and respond accordingly with challenge and support.

As the curriculum moves on, prior learning and intentional vocabulary remains accessible and is revisited, supporting retrieval as well as those children who develop at different rates. Children are empowered by the visual representation of their accumulation of experiences and knowledge.

In Key Stage 1, floorbooks have helped us to capture pupil utterances which demonstrate a depth and level of understanding that written work would not necessarily allow them to. This has been transformational for identifying pupil potential, particularly with our SEND pupils. Using them strengthens formative assessment as well as providing opportunities to explore links to other knowledge.

Revisiting past discussions allow teachers the opportunity to address misconceptions and, crucially, to plan for further challenge to embed a depth of understanding. Our children light up when they review their discussions and see their contributions!

Willow Primary School, Doncaster

Professional development opportunities in Doncaster have also been ideal moments to highlight the importance of children's voices in guiding daily routines and practice. Recent training devised by Abi Kershaw (Area SENCO) on Self-Regulation, Co-Regulation and Trauma Informed Approaches focuses on the importance of understanding how children are feeling when they attend our settings daily and how having regard to these feelings can shape how we interact with children in the coming day. This is a vital part of how we can put children's voices and wellbeing at the top of the agenda in all we do.

Opportunities in newsletters and through 'Equity and Diversity' training also demonstrate ways to represent the voices of neurodivergent children in settings, by using books and stories to read with children and advocate a neurodiversity-affirming approach for children.

Over recent months in Doncaster, we have learned more about the importance of listening to and acting on the voices of children through their physical body language and range of communication. This has provided our team an opportunity to reflect on staple strategies previously recommended, presumed as a way to enable children to have increased access to learning opportunities, but which through a different lens are compliant based. This has opened a dialogue with providers to carefully consider whether strategies are used to try to make neurodivergent children more neurotypical or whether the strategy is well placed to promote a child's autonomy and voice.

Recently, a provider in the north of Doncaster sought advice on this issue. The educators had started to question some of their practice and had reflected that some of their routines may be compliance based rather than neurodiversity affirming. We spoke specifically about group times and expectations. The educators were beginning to reflect on their expectations for all children to sit to access story/songs. They reflected that outcomes in children's personalised plans were sometimes set to achieve the action of *sitting* rather than *engagement*.

We discussed changing outcomes and routines to focus on engagement – for example, previous outcome: child will sit for five minutes for carpet time; new outcome: child will show engagement in story time and song time by multimodal communication – joining in with actions, moving to music, lycra, props, parachute play, using echolalia to repeat a character name or phrase from a story in play. We discussed the problems with presuming that engagement was shown through sitting, maintaining eye contact (neurotypical behaviours) and the advantages of being open to how engagement may present differently for neurodivergent children.

The setting shared with me:

> Staff are really beginning to think about the strategies through a different lens and focus more on the autonomy of the child, their learning style and their voice. After attending training and following discussion with the Early Years Inclusion Team, we have reflected on how we increase engagement through the experiences we offer and not to presume that engagement presents the same for every child.
>
> Doncaster Early Years Setting

Going back to the outcome and placing emphasis on what would be beneficial experiences for the individual child really helped us to reflect on whether outcomes were promoting compliance or valuing the child's voice and autonomy. For some settings, this brought up more questions than answers, but, as I reflected with many educators, being on the journey of reflection and positioning ourselves to learn more means that we are already committing to advocating for individual children's voices and how we can change practice to uphold these.

Thought Provocations

- How do you enable a child's 'voice' in your setting or school?
- Is every child's voice valued?

References

Cowan, K. & Flewitt. R. (2021) Moving from paper-based to digital documentation in Early Childhood Education: Democratic potentials and challenges. *International Journal of Early Years Education* *31*(4), 888–906. https://doi.org/10.1080/09669760.2021.2013171

Child's Name

Child's Voice

Where possible, this space should be completed in conjunction with the child. Consider alternative communication approaches to enable the child to contribute as fully as possible. The adult completing this page should know the child very well.

What I love to do:

What I dislike:

My aspirations:

Copyright material from Ann Lowe and Stephen Kilgour (2025), *The Inclusive Early Years Educator*, Routledge

Chapter 11

PARENTS' VIEWS AND ASPIRATIONS

As educators, it can be all too easy to fall into the trap of criticising parents and families, especially if the family in question has raised concerns about the quality of your provision in some way. As we know, the job of an early years educator or leader can be stressful and challenging, just like the role of a parent. Add into the mix that we are looking after a family's most precious gift, and it is easy to see why communications can sometimes become tense.

The source of issues can usually be categorised into one of the following:

- The family believes that the school or setting is not offering a high enough standard of care/education.
- The school or setting believes that the family is overly fussy/interfering.
- The school or setting believes that the family is not carrying out its responsibilities correctly.

Once these opinions have been established, it can be difficult (but not impossible) to get home–setting relations back on track. The best way of avoiding these scenarios is to seek to establish genuinely high-quality communications from day one. Unfortunately, there are situations where a child's family does not have the best of intentions for a child's welfare, but in the vast majority of situations this is not the case. Obviously, if there are ever concerns of this nature, safeguarding procedures should be followed. The support of a good setting or school in these particular scenarios can be hugely beneficial to the child in question.

There are also situations where it might appear that a family does not have the best of intentions for the child's welfare, but what is actually happening is that they struggling to cope. The impact of support from a good setting or school in these circumstances cannot be underestimated.

DOI: 10.4324/9781003409618-12

Regardless of what has or hasn't happened in terms of home–school/setting relations, we should never lose sight of the fact that, in the vast majority of cases, the family of a child will know them better than anyone else. As inclusive educators, tapping into this knowledge can be so powerful – helping us to provide the best possible education and care for the child. The benefit of having high-quality relationships with families can also not be underestimated. On top of day-to-day information sharing, if efforts have been made to establish a strong rapport with a family, then resolutions to problems, if they do arise, are much more likely.

Initial Meetings

The adage 'you don't get a second chance to make a first impression' can be very true in the early years. A family needs to have an instant feeling of safety and trust in the people who are going to be looking after their child, particularly if they are very young. The last thing a family wants when they visit for the first time is a chaotic experience, but as anyone who has worked in education can attest, moments of chaos can occur and often when you least want them to! Ensuring we are well prepared for visits can mean that we have the best possible chance of avoiding moments like this. The obvious things like scheduling appointments at times when we know we are well staffed and transitions aren't taking place can be a good start. On top of that, investing time in finding out more about the child in advance of their visit can be very beneficial – especially if a child has learning differences or a disability. Reading notes on a child can help us to plan a visit effectively. If, for example, we are aware an autistic child who has noise sensitivities is visiting, how can we make adjustments on the day to ensure that distress will be minimised?

Making appropriate time available on the day of a family's visit is also very important. This is easier said than done in a busy setting or school, but the significance of not feeling rushed or not feeling like an inconvenience cannot be downplayed. We should be genuinely interested in finding out about a family and child, and if we are, this will be clear to everyone involved.

The information contained in Chapter 4 on anti-racist practice is particularly important when meeting families for the first time. Does your setting or school feel inclusive and welcoming to all? Will families feel a sense of belonging as they are shown around? If not, adjustments are needed. Honesty and openness are key, especially if you are only just getting started on your anti-racist journey. If, for example, your staff team is lacking in terms of representation and diversity, don't be afraid to talk about this. Explain the hopes you have for the future based on what you now understand and are continuing to learn.

Home Visits

When you are well versed in visiting family homes as part of your nursery or school induction programme, it can be easy to forget the significance of this event for families. It can also be easy to fall into the trap of carrying out the type of visits that mean the process is as quick as possible, in order to fit the required amount into your busy working week. As much as we can, we need to give time to enhance the personalisation and humanisation of these experiences so that families aren't made to feel that these visits are an inconvenience.

The first step in truly valuing home visits is to reflect on the positive impact they have on a child's settling and learning. In my experience, there is a risk that home visits can become 'tick boxy'. This feeling is generally enhanced when there is a form that needs to be completed. The process can quite quickly begin to feel like a robotic interview or, worse still, an interrogation. The risk of the event feeling stressful for a family may be enhanced if they have cultural or language differences from the educator making the visit. We must always attend with sensitivity and respect at the heart of our thinking.

There is some information that is essential to gather when a child is about to start with you. It is therefore impossible to carry out a home visit without some non-negotiable questions (allergies, known professionals, etc.), but can we reflect on the rest of our questions and see if we can make these more open and warm? In the Educator's View section below, Professor Eunice Lumsden advocates this opening question when meeting parents for the first time: 'Can you tell me about your child's name? Why did you choose it?' This is obviously not a crucial line of questioning, but it shows you have noticed and are interested, and it may mean a family relaxes a little and gives you an insight into their thinking. Try to focus on positives and what brings the family and child joy. This is increasingly important if a child has learning differences or a disability, where the family is likely to have multiple experiences of deficit language and viewpoints.

We should also respond to cues, whether they be verbal or non-verbal. If, for example, a parent seems to become upset or looks uncomfortable, it might not be appropriate to continue the visit. It is also worth considering that the visit may have caused significant anxiety in advance. Educators are rightly held in high esteem by many families, and this can be amplified in different cultures. It is a big deal to welcome a professional into your home, especially when it is likely that judgements will be made, whether consciously or unconsciously. Always proceed with sensitivity, kindness and understanding.

Using Information

It would be hoped that having completed setting and home visits, an educator will be in a good position to welcome a child for the first time. We should make certain that we have shared the necessary information gathered with anyone working with the child, and consider whether our provision needs adjustments based on what we have learned about them. It should be clear if a child has any special interests, and it would be sensible to use this to our advantage in those initial few days. If a child has learning differences, it is likely that a support plan or Education, Health and Care Plan may be in place, and a family's views should be central to any document of this nature.

Ongoing Involvement

It is so important that a parent's views and aspirations continue to be valued throughout a child's time in our care. Settings and schools need to cultivate opportunities for continued dialogue around all aspects of a child's life, be that their general wellbeing, significant life events (e.g. a new sibling) or progress across curriculum areas. Not only do we need to gather these views, but we need to seek ways of enhancing our provision based on them. As inclusive educators, we must value what a family tells us about their child.

Educator's View – Eunice Lumsden (Professor of Child Advocacy and Head of Childhood Youth and Families at the University of Northampton)

One of the greatest pleasures of working with Early Childhood students in higher education is watching them begin to question, critique and develop their practice. I particularly enjoy engaging in discussions about working with families and unpicking the term 'Parent Partnership', which is a central theme of the EYFS in England.

There are two questions I suggest should be asked at the very start of the journey, when parents and carers come to see if your setting is right for their child:

- Can you tell me about your child's name? Why did you choose it?
- What are your hopes for your child?

The follow-on question is:

- How can we work together to ensure your child develops the knowledge and skills they need?

These questions shape different conversations that start with the child and their family. They embrace differences, promote inclusivity in our work and lay the foundations for future working. They also:

- recognise that all families are different
- understand that parents have hopes and dreams for their children
- enable different conversations about the experiences the child will have in the setting and the skills these will develop
- embrace what research tells us about the importance of both parents and the 'home learning' environment for educational outcomes.

Underpinning these questions is the knowledge and skills those working with children and families require. These include knowledge about family life, the importance of the family in child development and the ability to communicate and listen.

Developing a Reflective Approach to Parent Partnerships in Doncaster

In Doncaster, working in partnership with families is upheld as the key to achieving improved outcomes for children. There is a special quality about the way that the communities work together in Doncaster and support each other. I began in Chapter 1 talking about the way early years providers went over and above to meet the needs of families during flooding and during the pandemic, selfless and generous in their approach. This is a characteristic embodied in so many people, providers and early years educators in Doncaster, and evident when I visit settings, schools and family hubs. In the examples below, I share just a snapshot of some of the work taking place – there are many, many ways this work is developing, continuing to put family aspirations at the heart of the work we do.

Reflecting on the Importance of Parent Partnerships – A Case Study

Seedlings is an award-winning specialist provision in the north of Doncaster, winning Pre-School of the Year at the Nursery World Awards in 2023 and rated as Outstanding. It is a specialist nursery for children aged 2–4 years with an identified special educational need and/or disability, who can access the provision without an Education, Health and Care Plan or diagnosis.

Professionals or parents can make a referral to Seedlings. If a place is allocated, the first step is to get to know the family more and plan a bespoke transition process for each child. This is made up of a combination of suitable times for the family to visit the nursery and home visits by the nursery educators to the family home. This allows for the setting to plan a bespoke transition for the child, involving flexible visits to home and setting, and matching the child with a key worker who will support them in the nursery, as well as begin the processes for children to have the support they need when transitioning to school. Parents' views and aspirations are particularly important to gather in these early stages of a child transitioning to the setting.

It's so incredibly important to find out parents' views and aspirations for every child starting at a setting, but even more so for children who are neurodivergent. Parents of neurodivergent children have often experienced a number of barriers already in these very early years of their child's life. Often when children start at Seedlings, they have never accessed a consistent provision or playgroup before. During visits, the Seedlings team find out as much information as possible about the individual child: what regulates them, if they have any sensory sensitivities, how they communicate, what they are interested in and much more.

Parents hold the most knowledge about their child, and home visits/visits to Seedlings before starting allow for this knowledge to be shared and the beginning of a relationship to be forged. Parents often describe the difficulties they have experienced in taking their child to playgroups or provisions, many saying how hard it is to find somewhere/someone who could meet their child's needs. Often parents want somewhere they feel their child will be happy and cared for, and someone to hear them, support them and advocate for their child.

Emma Cammack, Special Education Needs Development Officer and Seedlings Educator, describes the importance of gathering parents' views and developing parent relationships in Seedlings before a child begins at the setting:

Within Seedlings, we recognise and support parents as their child's first and most important educators and welcome them into the life of the nursery. We are committed to working in partnership with all families, to provide a consistent and continuous level of care between home and nursery; this is embedded into our practice.

We strongly believe that parents and staff need to work together in close partnership for children to receive a quality of care and early learning opportunities, to meet their individual needs and support them to become strong, independent learners. We welcome parents as partners and support a two-way sharing of information that helps establish trust and understanding. We are committed to supporting parents in an open and sensitive manner to include them as an integral part of the care and learning within the nursery.

Prior to a child commencing at Seedlings and throughout their time at our nursery, we listen to and support parents to develop their confidence and encourage them to trust their own instincts and judgement regarding their child and their individual needs. It is also important, however, to have open and honest conversations to establish if further intervention may be needed to support the family as a whole. Ongoing communications between nursery and parents supports positive collaborative working when implementing the right support for their child, at the right place and at the right time.

Prior to professionals submitting a referral for a placement at Seedlings, we advise that parents visit the nursery as well as other mainstream/specialist provisions with their child. This allows parents to make an informed decision, to effectively meet the needs of their child. During this visit, detailed information can then be obtained regarding the child's primary need, current professional involvement and any intervention the child may require to support their learning and development.

During the child's initial visit, we obtain the aspirations, needs and expectations of parents. We continue to do this through regular feedback via questionnaires, a suggestion system and encouraging parents to review working practices. We evaluate any responses and publish these for parents with an action plan to inform future policy and staff development. This ensures the parent's and child's voices/opinions are heard and considered throughout.

Emma Cammack (Seedlings Educator and
Special Educational Needs Development Officer)

Establishing this parent partnership is vital to plan for the next steps in a child's education. Once their child is approaching statutory school age, parents will need to make decisions about which school they feel is the best fit for their child. Establishing a shared dialogue through listening and talking to parents about their views and aspirations for their child is paramount for their key person. Many of these discussions can be fostered in Assess, Plan, Do, Review meetings and when devising personalised plans for individual children. This also enables the key person and parents to work on joint outcomes at home and in Seedlings.

Nicola Wosman, Special Education Needs Development Officer and Seedlings Educator, shares how parents' views are gathered through Assess, Plan, Do, Review meetings prior to a child accessing their Reception school place:

During the autumn term Assess, Plan, Do, Review (APDR) meeting, prior to the child being statutory school age, the key person will begin transition discussions to ascertain parents' wishes and aspirations. Upon listening to parents' wishes, the key person will support them to visit mainstream and specialist provisions to allow the parents to make an informed decision as to what school they would like their child to attend that best meets their needs and will allow them to continue to thrive. A multiagency partnership approach is adopted where professionals are invited to the APDR meeting to support parents further – for example, educational psychology, occupational therapy, speech and language therapy and health visiting.

During this meeting, it may also be discussed whether a request for an Education, Health and Care Plan is to be completed to support the child's transition into mainstream or specialist provision. Once a school place has been confirmed within the spring term, an APDR meeting is held with the school and professionals to complete a robust transition plan to ensure the child's transition to school is smooth and successful. This includes support visits, role-modelling strategies and sharing current learning outcomes with the key person prior to the child's transition, as well as support once they commence their new placement.

Nicola Wosman (Special Education Needs
Development Officer and Seedlings Educator)

In Doncaster, we are keen to develop more professional development opportunities for early years educators in this area. Lisa Hill (Special Educational Needs Development Officer) and Tracy Outram (Team Manager for SENDIAS) have started to plan training opportunities to offer more support and guidance for educators to enable improved partnership working with parents. In beginning to plan CPD in this area, Lisa and Tracey spoke about the difficulties many parents face in understanding the graduated approach, the SEND Code of Practice, their rights as parents and the importance of listening and supporting parents to achieve shared outcomes.

A starting point is understanding their aspirations for their child and how early years settings start conversations to uphold these. Lisa Hill, Special Educational Needs Development Officer and parent of a child with SEND, describes the progress we are making as a sector:

> There are so many barriers for parents, and they need as much help and support as they can get. The number of barriers I have faced over the many years has been phenomenal. What I do like is that times are changing for the better and parents have a much louder voice now, more than ever, and we are supporting them to be heard even more.
>
> Lisa Hill (Special Educational Needs Inclusion Officer and parent of a child with SEND)

We are committed to increasing partnership working between early years providers and parents in Doncaster. Developing this from the lived experience of parents with children with SEND helps to increase our understanding of the support parents benefit from and how to reduce barriers. What we know is that by working in partnership with parents, we can achieve the best possible outcomes for every child.

Thought Provocations

- Do you make enough time to establish high-quality relationships with families?
- Are there adjustments that could be made to your transition processes – particularly when a child is going to be starting with you?

Child's Name

Parents' Views and Aspirations

Providers should talk to parents and families about their aspirations for their child to empower them to play a central role in making decisions about their child's education and care.

These partnerships are the key to a successful early years experience for children.

Parents and providers should plan support and interventions together that will recognise parents' aspirations through long-term targets, objectives for the next phase of education and targets for the next half or full term.

Life aspirations for my child:

Long-term aspirations (two years):

Short-term next steps (this year):

Copyright material from Ann Lowe and Stephen Kilgour (2025), *The Inclusive Early Years Educator*, Routledge

ADDITIONAL FORMS

Holistic Reflection Overview

Consider your reflections completed throughout the workbook and identify your main priorities by completing the holistic overview below.

There is an outer circle and three inner circles, giving you four options to choose from. The outer circle denotes that there are no barriers in this area and that the child's needs in this area are met – if this is your reflection, mark all four sections.

The innermost circle denotes that there are significant barriers in this area and removing them should be prioritised when considering next steps of action and provision for the child.

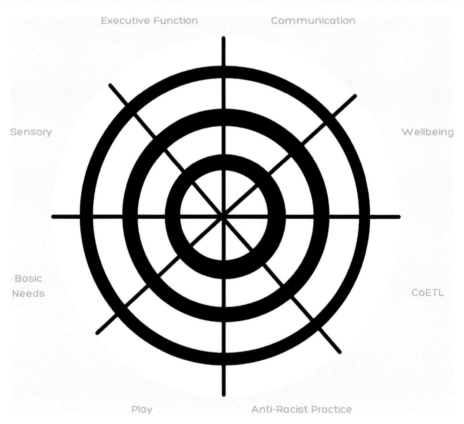

Holistic Reflection Overview

Copyright material from Ann Lowe and Stephen Kilgour (2025), *The Inclusive Early Years Educator*, Routledge

Goals

These goals should be child-centred and a collaboration between the child, the family and relevant professionals. Reflect upon the priorities identified throughout the workbook when setting new goals.

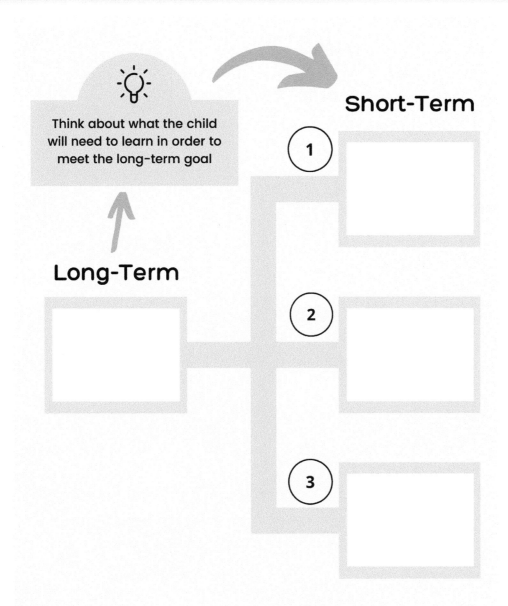

Think about what the child will need to learn in order to meet the long-term goal

Short-Term

1

2

3

Long-Term

Copyright material from Ann Lowe and Stephen Kilgour (2025), *The Inclusive Early Years Educator*, Routledge

Child's Name

Progress Towards Outcomes

Use these spaces to periodically update how a child is progressing towards their individual outcomes. It may be useful to date your entries.

Short-term 1:

Short-term 2:

Short-term 3:

Long-term:

Copyright material from Ann Lowe and Stephen Kilgour (2025), *The Inclusive Early Years Educator*, Routledge

Child's Name

Actions

Use this space to write down any actions that are necessary as a result of your reflections. It might be useful to add dates and when they will be reviewed.

Copyright material from Ann Lowe and Stephen Kilgour (2025), *The Inclusive Early Years Educator*, Routledge

Child's Name

Extra Notes

Use this space to write any extra information that would be useful, or to continue from another page. It may be useful to add dates to your notes.

Copyright material from Ann Lowe and Stephen Kilgour (2025), *The Inclusive Early Years Educator*, Routledge

INDEX

Note: *Italic* page numbers refer to *figures* and **Bold** page numbers refer to **tables.**

Taylor & Francis Group
an **informa** business

Taylor & Francis eBooks

www.taylorfrancis.com

A single destination for eBooks from Taylor & Francis
with increased functionality and an improved user
experience to meet the needs of our customers.

90,000+ eBooks of award-winning academic content in
Humanities, Social Science, Science, Technology, Engineering,
and Medical written by a global network of editors and authors.

TAYLOR & FRANCIS EBOOKS OFFERS:

A streamlined
experience for
our library
customers

A single point
of discovery
for all of our
eBook content

Improved
search and
discovery of
content at both
book and
chapter level

REQUEST A FREE TRIAL
support@taylorfrancis.com

 Routledge
Taylor & Francis Group

 CRC Press
Taylor & Francis Group

*For Product Safety Concerns and Information please contact
our EU representative GPSR@taylorandfrancis.com Taylor & Francis
Verlag GmbH, Kaufingerstraße 24, 80331 München, Germany*

T - #0197 - 090625 - C214 - 297/210/10 - PB - 9781032529912 - Gloss Lamination